247 Healing plants

for Children under 12 years

(with 981 possible remedies)

Compiled and written by: José Enrique Centén Martín

Legal deposit: M-005118/2018

Cover image: JECM

Dedicated to my children
Victor Nike and Séfora

The genesis

What better than food to cure or cure, is what I write in this book about natural remedies for children under 12 years, arose from a particular problem, the vegetations in a baby, vegetations that made her rest badly being notorious lack of sleep in the creature. Consulting specialists on this issue began the doubts, the pediatrician of a Medical Society advised to operate, we opted for a new pediatric consultation to confirm the advice and opted for Social Security. The doctor Social Security discouraged the operation for being of total anesthesia, and so young age the girl, told us that they were defenses, recommended waiting before going through surgery as usually, between 5 and 8 years the vegetation disappears. In the meantime, he advised us to maintain an optimum humidity level at night to alleviate vegetations, given that dry environments are harmful. We follow this second council and in turn decided to seek a natural remedy, in that search opened a huge range of plants and remedies against diseases and common ailments, until we found what could be the ideal for the "Vegetations", proved to be very effective, after 2 weeks the rest of the girl child improved as it eases the breathing through the mouth and almost disappear the hoarseness. After two months the problem is over, although in winter periods or a cold, it returns to routine, but spaced out in time or performed once a week.

Following the maxim of Hipócrates de Cós (460 - 370 BC) and given that in the smallest it is difficult in many cases the intake of the prescribed pharmacopoeia, rejected by system, and as we have all had herbal teas or infusions recommended by relatives and ancestors, I ventured to write a book, but not only herbal remedies, I have been more ambitious and opted for all kinds of known and unknown plants, in total 981, many with great benefits for our health, but without knowing how to use them efficiently, I hope that this book with its plants is a remedy for the problems we suffer, since for each disease there are several proposals and hardly any will not go well.

Presentation

"Let food be your food and food your medicine"

This monograph is part of the book 8256 of Natural Remedies a compendium of 801 plants, for the 170 most common ailments of the human body, **remedies, not universal panaceas,** able to alleviate the various ailments we suffer. The plants described are provided by the environment on different continents, but they are available to everyone due to commercial globalization. Many for everyday can surprise us its utility to be unknown by most people, others consume without knowing the extent of the benefit that could bring us if we used them for curative or preventive purposes. For the remedies Included for the remedies the **Water, Egg shell and Egg white,** being of everyday use in all households. I have also added the **Cremor of tartar** and **Pollen** derived from plants, but with obvious benefits. A specific section has been made: **Sweeteners,** necessary in the remedies to be beneficial to use in place the common refined sugar that does not contribute any.

With this book I intend to raise awareness of the value of each plant, and in some cases I was surprised to have them around us, that used in a rational manner, we can have a more healthy life and healthy and even preventive against possible greater evils.

They are remedies of popular use at first, but amply contrasted, remedies of plants unknown in their value, and possibly habituals in our environment or of everyday use without knowing its therapeutic benefits, many of them are even found in the rest of the world cultivated or as invasive due to a similar climatology.

The 247 plants here included among trees, flowers, fruits, herbs, vegetables, legumes, seeds..., **can be found in multiple forms of consumption:** dried or fresh, essences, syrups, in preparations such as ointments, tinctures, extracts dried or liquid In each plant is described the existence of **possible contraindications with diseases and drug interactions that are being taken at that time,** being necessary **to take into account** when consuming.

Also the plants can be used mixed being for the same utility, in order to potentiate a specific ailment, others, although without being of the same value or counterproductive can to mask flavors, especially in the little ones, always reluctant, two that do not usually fail are: Mint Piperita or **Vanilla** (with a drop of any vanilla preparation is enough).

In the utilization of the described plants they must watch especially their consumption: pregnant women, lactating mothers, children under 3 years of age and those with diabetes, hepatic, hypertensive, hypotensive, with chronic diseases, or taking medication for any other ailment. Plants in many cases can boost the drugs we are taking or be preventative for different ailments. **Never substitute a drug for a plant, and should also be monitored for antibiotic intake, there are plants that can decrease the absorption power of these, action that can make them ineffective.**

Ailments with number of remedies

When we choose any remedy in the ailment that we may suffer, it is always convenient to read the description of the plant to ensure possible contraindications or, interactions with medications you are taking. To consider that some plants could produce different discomfort, it should be taken into account so as not to be alarmed.

Children under 12 years of age

Never replace the medication by the natural remedies. These remedies are supported, **you should always consult with your child's doctor**.

Anemia - Reconstituents - Energizers

The smallest **are often reluctant to drink infusions, for their taste,** but they can be masked with mint, a drop of vanilla or any sweetener pleasant to your palate (see possible contraindications or interactions).

There are in the market sweeteners or syrups of different medicinal plants, choose the highest purity. **To avoid caries problems,** when using ingested infusions, it is advisable, if necessary, to sweeten, use any sweetener that is indicated in the **Sweeteners** section. I recommend low glycemic sweeteners, **less than 5%, for minors. ...Continue on next page**

... For diabetics, with diets and cholesterol problems, preferably **the Silver birch sugar of 0.2% and Stevia,** with no sugar, although with a slight taste of Liquorice.

- **Acorn,** as food is **energizing,** see **description of the plant.**

- **Agar Agar,** helps to prevent deficiency states and some types of anemia, although its caloric intake is almost nil the agar – agar provides important amounts of iron. **Reconstituent** containing phosphorus, essential for the nervous system in general **and for the correct transformation of sugars into energy,** see **description of the plant.**

- **Ajuga iva,** of excellent results against **anorexia** as a natural aperitif (better not to sweeten), see **description of the plant.**

- **Amaranth,** the iron contained in its leaves helps to prevent anemia, especially **in children,** see **description of the plant,** form of use **VIII.**

- **Anacahuita,** stimulant of the organism **(increases muscle energy),** see **description of the plant,** form of use **VII.**

- **Apple,** their regular consumption is good for **anemia.** Also **the juice** of apples, ½ glass of tomato juice, ½ glass of lemons, ½ glass of melon, drink three times a day, if it is strong to lower with honey and water, **Another beneficial way** is to mix the juicex of ¼ of apple and ¼ of beet, drink daily, see **the different descriptions of the plants.**

- **Banana,** its consumption **combat anemia** by providing a significant amount of iron, helping the formation of hemoglobin in the blood. Eating banana and orange (natural or in juice) in the first two years of life of our babies can **reduce the risk** of our children **develop leukemia.** It is convenient to consume for the protection of the **muscular mass** in infantile age **by the energetic wear** when being in continuous activity, see **description of the plant.**

- **Baobab tree,** great for cases of **anem ia** and excellent **restorative,** see **description of the plant.**

- **Barley,** good for the anti **anemic capacity** of chlorophyll, it contains folic acid, iron and copper, which favor and stimulate the synthesis of hemoglobin. It is **mineralizing and restorative,** especially for convalescence, due to its alkalizing power, by the content of vitamins and minerals. Also taken as water day, see **description of plant**, form of use **VII.**

- **Beet,** to combat anemia **daily drinking,** the mixture of the juices of ¼ of apple and a ¼ of beet, another way to combat it is eating cooked or raw. It contains iron, iodine, phosphorus, sodium, etc., occupying the main place among the vegetables **as a mineralising.** It is also used for **people in prostration to act as a restorative,** see **different descriptions of the plants.**

- **Bighead/Conehead thyme,** consume **your honey (from 1 year)** is good **for cases of anemia,** see **description of the plant.**

- **Bistort,** the infusion and liquefaction is good as a restorative, see **description of the plant**, forms of use **VII and IX.**

- **Black sesame,** the consumption of its oil is used to help prevent **anemia** due to its high iron content (9 mg), see **description of the plant.**

- **Black mulberry,** as a restorative the juice of the fruits is a refreshing and invigorating drink, which **helps in case of weakness,** see **description of the plant**

- **Bloodroot,** the infusion ingested for the treatment **of anemia,** see **description of the plant**, form of use **VII.**

- **Breckland thyme,** the infusion as a restorative aperitif is used against anemia, also in cases of **weakness and inappetence,** see **description plant.**

- **Brussels sprout,** its consumption to be rich in chlorophyll, helps combat anemia and the formation of hemoglobin. Its sulfur content is very high, it also contains arsenic, calcium, nitrogen and iodine, serves as an aperitif, **great source of minerals and restoratives,** see **description plant.**

- **Cacao,** tremendously energetic and **restorative** food, it helps **in physical efforts** to recover both physical and **mental** strength, being useful to keep us more active, see **description of the plant.**

- **Calabash or Pumpkin,** consumed raw mixed in salads, in soups and steamed, **is mineralizing** by its multiple properties, minerals and vitamins, antiscorbutic and refreshing, see **description of the plant.**

- **Carob tree,** its consumption prevents **anemia** by favoring the formation of red blood cells. Recommended in the smallest to be **energetic and restorative,** see **description of the plant.**

- **Chard,** regular consumption helps to avoid or fight anemia, being beneficial and essential. You can also drink a vegetable broth that is obtained by cooking common nettles, leeks, wild carrots, chard with water. The treatment lasts between three and six weeks and it is necessary to follow a diet to overcome the anemia, see **descriptions of the plants.**

- **Cherimoya,** its consumption provides iron, it favours the absorption of iron from food adequate against the **anemia,** see **description of the plant.**

- **Cherry/Cherrys tree,** the infusion of the leaves or stalks of the fruit is effective **against anemia,** see **description of the plant.**

- **Chestnut fruit,** its consumption is used to avoid **anemia,** because it is rich in iron, maintains a stronger health and thanks to its minerals the organism will be much healthier. Of **restorative and mineralizing** properties by the large amount of energy, all the proteins in addition to the minerals they present, among them: potassium, iron, phosphorus, magnesium, see **description of the plant.**

- **Chestnut tree,** as a **restorative** for cases of long convalescence, see **description of the plant,** form of use **VII (1).**

- **Chickpea,** being **energizing,** they must consume it from an early age due to their continuous physical exercises, see **description of the plant.**

- **Chives,** its consumption can be used in case of **anemia**, by stimulating the appetite, see **description of the plant. - Cinnamon,** the infusion is used in cases of anemia and anorexias to open the appetite, see **description of plant.**

- **Cinnamon with honey,** the warm infusion **from 1 year** is a highly calorific combination and works like a natural antibiotic. It expels the cold of the body and prevents diseases caused by viruses and bacteria. **Acts** as an **energizing tonic,** against exhaustion, spoonful of warm water or mixed with honey in the morning (preferably on an empty stomach) and a spoonful before going to bed. Its calorific and toning properties revitalize your body, see **description of the plant and of the Honey.**

- **Clary sage,** as **a restorative strengthens** the immune system, it is useful in the treatment of chronic fatigue syndrome. Restores and fortifies during **the convalescence** process, see **description of the plant.**

- **Coriander,** regular consumption is a good source of iron, fiber and magnesium that help fight **anemia,** see **description of the plant.**

- **Eggshell,** to use the **mineralizing** power of your calcium carbonate to soak eggshells with lemon juice for several days. Save the liquid in the refrigerator to add to juices of fruits and vegetables, see **description plant.**

- **Erythraea chilensis,** appetite stimulant ingested and helps in convalescence, see **description of the plant**, formof use **VII.**

- **Escarole,** its consumption is recommended in case of anemia. It is convenient in disorders of anorexia (loss of appetite), see **description of the plant.**

- **Evening primrose,** the oil is used as an **energizer or restorative,** treats the **post viral syndrome** that causes **dizziness,** see **description of the plant.**

- **Fenugreek,** consumed or in infusion favors the formation of red blood cells. **More than 100 gr. per day can cause ...Continue on next page**

...**diarrhea and nausea.** Powerful **restorative** that is administered in cases of lack of appetite, and benefits in case of anemia, see **description of the plant,** forms of use and consume **VII and VIII.**

- **Fiddle dock,** its consumption it is recommended **against anemia** because of its iron and vitamin C content, see **description of the plant.**

- **Green pepper,** its consumption by the potassium it contains is necessary for the transmission of nerve impulse and **muscle activity,** see **description of the plant.**

- **Grenadia,** excellent source of potassium, calcium, phosphorus and iron, **to prevent anemia,** see **description of the plant.**

- **Hazel,** the infusion is a good tonic **against anemia,** see **description of the plant,** form of use **VII.**

- **Hazelnut,** its consumption fights anemia and facilitates the absorption of iron to complement any deficiency. As **a mineralizer** it is very energetic, see **description of the plant.**

- **Heath speedwell,** the infusion ingested it is used regularly and indicated as an appetizer tonic in cases of **inappetence or lack of appetite** in the smallest, for **anaemia and as a restorative** by stimulating and increasing strength in cases of weakening of the body, see **description of the plant**

- **Herb Bennet,** it is used as a tonic against anemia and restorative, see **description of the plant**, forms of use **VII (1).**

- **Honey,** daily consumption **(from 1 year),** with water and an empty stomach fights fatigue and its symptoms in a matter of days, bring a lot of vitality keeping them more active, **being restorative,** see **description of the Honey.**

- **Hops,** the infusion ingested (any), having aperitif and antiseptic properties, useful to **stimulate the appetite** in inappetents, see **description of the plant**, form of use **VII.**

- **Jamaica pepper,** its consumption relieves the states of fatigue as **a restorative,** see **description of the plant.**

- **Jujube,** very convenient for anemia as restorative or in a serious state of prostration, see **description of the plant.**

- **Kale,** consume for being one of **the richest vegetable sources of iron,** makes it basic **for vegetarians and vegans,** thanks to this mineral **anemia is avoided,** see **description of the plant.**

- **Lamb´s lettuce, in english,** the consumption benefits the **anemic** and complications related to iron deficiency, see **description of the plant.**

- **Large-leaved lime,** la infusión **helps in recovering the appetite** after some gastrointestinal problem of the stomach. It can be **used to reinforce** the defenses by its vitamin C and **mineralizing** properties, see **description of the plant.**

- **Lemon,** good **for anemia,** combined with the juice of Apples, ½ glass of Tomato juice, ½ glass of Lemons, ½ glass of melon, drink three times a day, if it is strong to lower with honey and water, see **the different descriptions of the plants.**

- **Lentil,** its consumption is **very important against anemia,** rich in iron, a mineral used by the body for the production of red blood cells. **Beneficial** for the organs, and **for physical and muscular efforts,** as it requires a constant supply of proteins to function properly. **It is convenient as energizer** provides almost all of folic acid (vitamin B9), for an adult, useful for the proper functioning of the nervous system, in the production of energy and necessary for the synthesis of DNA, see **description of plant.**

- **Mango,** consumed regularly, being rich in iron, is useful for those who **suffer from anemia,** and to increase the number of red blood cells in the blood, see **description of the plant.**

- **Martagon lily,** it is used as a **restorative** for the treatment of fatigue, asthenias, see **description of the plant.**

- **Melon or Muskmelon,** good **for anemia,** combined with the juice of Apples, ½ glass of Tomato juice, ½ glass of Lemons, ½ glass of melon, drink three times a day, if it is strong to lower with honey and water, see **the different descriptions of the plants.**

- **Naranjilla,** its consumption rich in iron **ideal for the anemic,** it is recommended the regular consumption of naranjilla combined with egg, alfalfa and barley, exuberant calorie recipe, which helps considerably in weight gain, **being good mineralizing,** see **description of the plant.**

- **Nectarine,** its consumption by vitamin C is **recommended against anemia,** helping the body to absorb iron, see **description of the plant.**

- **Nettle,** it is used **against anemia** when the concentration of iron decreases in our blood, the lack of vitamins and minerals can be recovered by consuming nettles. The nettle offers, among other nutrients, calcium, silicon, zinc, copper, magnesium and at least 7 vitamins. To treat and reduce anemia you can drink a vegetable broth it is obtained by cooking nettles and other vegetables (Leek, Carrot, Chard) with water. The treatment lasts between three and six weeks and it is necessary to follow **a diet to overcome the anemia,** see **the different descriptions of plants.**

- **Niaouli,** the ingested infusion **(in older than 6 years),** also in topical use (in massage directly on the skin) is used to be **antibacterial, antiviral and anti-infectious,** see **description of the plant,** form of use **VII.**

- **Orange,** the ingested infusion of their leaves is very helpful if they have lost their **appetite,** in this case it is best to give them an infusion on an empty stomach for several days. Its consumption is very adequate due to its great mineralizing effect, see **description of the plant.**

- **Oregano,** the infusion **ingested** it is used as **a restorative** and in the face of inappetence, see **description of the plant,** form of use **VII.**

- **Parsley,** its consumption is ideal for people with **anemia, fatigue and physical tiredness, as a restorative,** for its richness in minerals, by providing interesting amounts of iron, phosphorus and calcium, see **description of the plant.**

- **Passion fruit,** consumption prevents **anemia** because its properties favor the absorption of iron from food, see **description of the plant.**

- **Pea,** food **anti anemic** for its content in iron and vitamins of group B, see **description of the plant.**

- **Peach,** its consumption **(moderate in children under 6 years),** is recommended for **cases of anemia** and as **a restorative** for weakness and fatigue states, see **description of the plant.**

- **Pineapple,** because of its high percentage of carbohydrates **is energizing,** the juice like fruit, see **description of the plant.**

- **Pollen,** it counteracts possible nutritional deficiencies, especially during periods of high physiological demand, such as **anemia.** Efficient in situations of physical exhaustion **as restorative,** for its invigorating and stimulating effect, even of notorious euphoriant, see **description of the Pollen,** forms of use **VIII (2 and 3).**

- **Pomegranate,** rich in iron, is indicated for those who **suffer from anemia,** see **description of the plant,** form of use **VIII.**

- **Potato,** its consumption it is convenient because they can **provide energy** to our organism, see **description of the plant.**

- **Prunus,** the infusion of the flowers, ingested, is a good tonic, stimulating as a **restorative** against fatigue and **anemia,** see **description of the plant.**

- **Psoralea,** the infusion ingested as **a restorative aperitif** and to whet your appetite, see **description of the plant**, form of use **VII.**

- **Quinua,** its consumption is very convenient to fight **anemia** and **as a mineralizer,** as it contains magnesium, potassium, zinc and iron, see **description of the plant.**

- **Raisin grape,** its consumption fights **anemia,** being a rich source of protein and iron, see **description of the plant.**

- **Rice,** the liquid of its decoction used as day water, is very effective as **energetic,** see **description of the plant.**

- **Roquet,** its consumption is beneficial as a good **mineralizing** to contains some basic minerals for the functioning of the organism (potassium, phosphorus and manganese), see **description of the plant.**

- **Rowan,** the berries or their juice helps **the anemic** for its vitaminic properties and to increase the appetite. Juice is a good restorative for weakness **after serious illnesses** and long convalescence, see **description of the plant**, formof use **VII (2).**

- **Salep drink,** its consumption is a natural **toning restorative,** ideal for **convalescents, asthenic, in** cases of fatigue, see **description of the plant.**

- **Sanicle,** ingested combat **anemia, and restorative** against fatigue and physical weakness, see **description of the plant.**

- **Soursop,** the mixture of leaves and a handful of flowers is used to treat **states of convalescence,** illness that weakens or after an operation, as **restorative and energizing,** see **description of the plant.**

- **Spinach,** convenient for the nitrates present in spinach, these are responsible for increasing **the strength in the muscles, ...Continue**

.. they regulate oxygen according to demand when they come into action and help to increase **muscle mass** due to its high protein content. The enzymes called cytochromes, which have the group heme or heme (iron) in their composition gives **mineralizing properties, see description plant.**

- **Spirulina**, its consumption is used with **very positive effects on children** with malnutrition in combination with the usual food, **it is not a substitute.** The **energy contribution** of spirulina is suitable for people with a high wear on the physical level **as restorative,** see **description of the plant.**

- **Strawberries,** the ingested infusion is good tonic against **anemia** and to fight **anorexia.** It has a **restorative,** fortifying and regenerating action on the organism in cases of weakness, convalescence of diseases, see **description of the plant**, form of use **VII.**

- **Sugarcane,** the liquefaction ingested as an aperitif is a good **restorative** tonic. Good source of glucose as **energizing,** helps to rehydrate the body giving a boost of energy in **physical efforts,** see **description of the plant,** form of use **IX.**

- **Sunflower,** consume as **a restorative** because it contains a lot of potassium and magnesium, see **description of the plant.**

- **Tamarind,** the infusion ingested due to their healthy sugars they provide energy being **good restorative,** and a **very beneficial serum** combined with mineral water, salt and brown sugar, see **description of the plant**, form of use **VII.**

- **Tomato,** its consumption is good for **anemia** combined the juice of Apples, ½ glass of Tomato juice, ½ glass of Lemons, ½ glass of Melon, drink three times a day, see **the different descriptions of the plants.**

- **Walnut tree / Nut,** the ingested infusion of its leaves is used to combat the generalized physical **weakening** as a restorative, against **anemia,** see **description of the plant,** form of use **VII.**

- **West Indian cherry,** this fruit should be consumed by **remineralizing** for multiple indications such as growth, recovery of asthenia or of states of great weakness, see **description of the plant.**

- **Wheat,** consumption for your B vitamins helps metabolize food and **convert it into energy. As a mineralizer** it is excellent for its variety of vitamins and minerals, see **description of the plant.**

- **White horehound,** the infusion ingested is used to combat anaemia and body weakness as a **restorative,** see **description of the plant.**

- **White Chilean myrtle,** the infusion of its leaves, ingested, stimulates the appetite in case of **anemia,** see **description of the plant.**

- **White nettle,** the infusion ingested of the flowers and tips flowery or cooked combat **anemic deficiencies,** and **as restorative,** see **description of the plant**, forms of use an cosume **VII and VIII.**

- **White pepper,** the consumption **(only cooked in powder),** because of its high iron content makes the pepper white help **prevent anemia** caused by lack of iron, see **description of the plant.**

- **Yam,** for **over 6 years,** as a **restorative** in cases of **general fatigue and apathy,** see **description of the plant.**

- **Finally,** we describe the plants that only **the simple infusion is necessary to ingest** as tonics, being good to stimulate appetite and combat cases of anemia the following plants:

Gum arabic tree, Loosestrife, Mountain everlasting, Patience dock, Spiked loosestrife, Thyme, Yellow trumpetbush.

If the infusion is going to be **used frequently,** recommend **boiling the plant in a liter of water, or in the amount of water that we create** according to the daily use to be taken, thus way we will avoid time in its preparation and instead of the prepared bags that they sell you can buy in bulk to economize. It can **also be potentiated** with ... **Continue on next page**

... different plants for the same ailment, but it is convenient **to always remember** the perfect use of each plant used according **to its description,** in case there is any **interaction with drugs or posible.**

Antibacterials - Antibiotics - Flu

Never replace the medication by the natural remedies. These remedies are supported, **you should always consult with your child's doctor**.

To avoid caries problems, when using ingested infusions, it is advisable, if necessary, to sweeten, use any sweetener that is indicated in the **Sweeteners** section.

- **Asafoetida,** plant root compounds can kill H1N1, **swine flu virus.** It also acts in the **seasonal flu,** see **description of the plant.**

- **Ash,** the infusion ingested as antipyretic, to **lower the fever** and as a remedy against **the flu,** see **description of the plant.**

- **Baccharises,** extraordinary **antibacterial,** by keeping the body clean and healthy, see **description of the plant**, form of use **VII (1).**

- **Bay laurel,** the infusion ingested contains substances with **anti-bactericidal** action, see **description of the plant.**

- **Beet,** consume cooked helps fight with the negative of the environment, as **antibacterial,** by resisting the microbes and bacteria in the organism, see **description of the plant.**

- **Black mulberry,** when consuming the fruit, it acts as **an antibacterial** because it contains alkaloids that activate macrophages (white blood cells that stimulate the immune system and put on active alert against threats to our molecular health), see **description of the plant.**

- **Blue agave,** the infusion ingested as an **antibacterial** that favors the growth of good bacteria decreases the growth of other pathogens that generate toxic compounds, see **description of the plant.**

- **Broadleaf plantain,** the infusion ingested or the consumption **of its seeds** are used **as antibacterial,** see **description of plant,** form of use **VII.**

- **Brussels sprout,** great detoxifying and **antibacterial** of our organism, see **description of the plant.**

- **Carob tree,** effective for the functioning of **the immune and antibacterial system** by its high content of vitamins A, of group B (B1, B2, B3, B6, B9 or folic acid), see **description of the plant.**

- **Catnip,** the infusion ingested it is used as **an antibiotic,** see **description of the plant**.

- **Chachacoma,** la infusión ingerida is used in the **flu processes,** see **description of the plant**, form of use **VII.**

- **Chalk milkwort,** it is used in infusion to fight **the flu,** see **description of the plant.**

- **Cherimoya,** fruit source of vitamin A and C has **antioxidant effect,** increases red blood cells and resistance to infections, **as antibacterial,** see **description of the plant.**

- **Chives,** consumption as an **antibacterial** favors the elimination of toxins from the body to fight infections. It increases and stimulates, as a form of **antibiotic,** the immune system, see **description of the plant.**

- **Cinnamon with honey,** this combination **from 1 year** is highly calorific and works **as a natural antibiotic.** It expels the cold of the body and prevents diseases caused by viruses and bacteria, see **description of the plant and of the Honey.**

- **Clementine,** its consumption for its **antibacterial** properties, they avoid risk of infectious diseases and **the flu** so normal in autumn, see **description of the plant.**

- **Coriander,** its consumption improves the immune system by possessing **antibacterial properties,** avoiding the proliferation of the Salmonella virus in food, see **description of the plant.**

- **Cornflower,** the infusion is a potent **antibiotic,** helps in cases of infections combining its antibiotic properties with desinflamative and antipyretic, see **description of the plant**, form of use **VII.**

- **Echinacea,** it is the **natural antibiotic** par excellence for all types of infections, and in general to **promote** the **immune system,** to increase the defenses of the organism, boost the immune system, capable of activating our production of leukocytes, you can even take a daily infusion without fear as **a preventive, there are preparations for over 6 years,** see description of the plant.

- **Erythraea chilensis,** in infusions or as day water is of **antibiotic effect and antioxidant.** To treat the flu is effective to drink hot or as day water, see **description of the plant**, form of use **VII.**

- **Escarole,** its consumption it is suitable **as antibacterial** against situations that increase the infections, see **description of the plant.**

- **Eucalyptus,** in vapours or infusion as **an antibacterial** manages to kill those microorganisms causing infectious processes in the respiratory tract, see **description of the plant.**

- **Fiddle dock,** consume as an **antibacterial preventive,** see **description of the plant.**

- **Garden nasturtium,** the infusion or decoction is considered a **natural antibiotic,** see **description of the plant**, forms of use **VII.**

- **Garlic,** consumption in brine or cooked is good antibacterial, and almost a **natural antibiotic.** It is advised in the coldest times of the year, when it is common to get sick with **colds or flu,** see **description of the plant.**

- **Grapefruit,** its consumption as **antibacterial** is effective because of its high content in flavonoids and vitamin C stimulates the functions of the immune system, see **description of the plant.**

- **Hazel,** relieves the fever. It is an effective remedy **against the flu,** see **description of the plant**, form of use **VII.**

- **Helychrysum,** ingested to be **antibacterial** improves the functioning of the metabolism, see **description of the plant.**

- **Honey,** a spoonful of **water and fasting daily,** is a great remedy that increases the defenses as **antibacterial** and almost **antibiotic,** and prevents the organism **against the flu,** see **description of the Honey.**

- **Honeysuckle,** the infusion is used as a successful **antibacterial** in internal infections and for the **treatment of flu,** see **description of plant.**

- **Iceland moss,** the double decoction ingested by its content of uric acid and polycystic acid, substances responsible for its activity **as an antibiotic,** see **description of the plant,** form of use **VII.**

- **Jasmine,** drinking jasmine tea is good for its antiviral and **antibacterial** properties. also **ingested and gargle** can prevent **the flu,** and helps to have an earlier recovery, see **description of the plant.**

- **Jew's ear,** its consumption it acts as **a good antibiotic** helping to cure tumors of the whole body, see **description of the plant.**

- **Kaki fruit,** good **antibacterial** for vitamin C, helps to strengthen the immune system, in fact, when the body fights against an infection, the daily requirements of this vitamin can be multiplied by 10. ... **Continue**

... Effective in the **prevention of flu** due to its contribution in vitamins A and C in joint action, see **description of the plant.**

- **Kale,** its consumption is beneficial for its vitamin C when activating the immune system **as antibacterial** and beneficial for the **stomach metabolism,** see **description of the plant.**

- **Kiwi,** its consumption as **antibacterial** due to folic acid combined with its contribution of vitamin C, collaborates in the production of red and white blood cells and in the formation of antibodies **that favor the immune system.** In cases **of iron deficiency anemia** due to its vitamin C, it increases the absorption of iron from food, see **description of the plant.**

- **Kudzu,** it is convenient to consume **as an antibacterial** when it is used as an attack against the daily microbes and to alleviate problems in the processes related **to flu,** see **description of the plant.**

- **Large-leaved lime,** the infusion ingested it has antibacterial and **antiviral** properties acting on occasion **as a natural antibiotic,** see **description of the plant.**

- **Leek,** its consumption can act as an **antibiotic,** excellent for the health of the little ones, see **description of the plant.**

- **Lemon,** its consumption it is good **for flu-like conditions**, by providing vitamin C, see **description of the plant.**

- **Lemon grass,** the infusion ingested, **use the bags already** made, has **antibacterial properties,** see **description of the plant.**

- **Lilac,** the infusion ingested of the bark or flowers is good in the **flu processes,** see **description of the plant.**

- **Linden tree,** for its properties on the sweat glands (flavonoglucosides), as carminative and diaphoretic is used to be effective against **flu processes,** see **description of the plant**, form of use **VII.**

- **Loquat,** the infusion ingested or the extract the leaves of the tree to be **antibacterial** potentiate the immune system. Also the consumption of its fruit, see **description of the plant.**

- **Malabar nut,** the infusion ingested of the whole plant, **in older than 3 years,** as **an antibacterial** and good **antioxidant,** see **description of plant.**

- **Mountain everlasting,** very effective and as an antibiotic, particularly for cases of **anthrax,** see **description of the plant.**

- **Mouse-ear hawkweed,** the infusion ingested it is useful **in older than 3 years** for the **flu processes.** It is recommended its **juice** by possessing **antibiotic and anti-infectious** properties to treat brucellosis, see **description of the plant.**

- **Myrrh,** the infusion is used as **an antibacterial** for its antimicrobial power, and useful **in seasonal flu,** see **description of the plant.**

- **Myrtle,** the infusion ingested **(in older than 6 years),** it is used to contain compounds such as Pineneo, Cineol, Dipenteno, Mirtol and Mirtenol, properties compared to those of penicillin, it **is antibacterial** and almost a natural **antibiotic,** see **description of the plant**, form of use **VII.**

- **Naranjilla,** its consumption allows the whole organism to remain immune to being an **effective antibacterial** the immune system, see **description of the plant.**

- **Niaouli,** to clean and disinfect **minor wounds,** pour 5 or 6 drops in 250 ml of boiled water, use cooled or tempered. Ingested infusion **(in older than 6 years)** to treat **the flu,** see **description of the plant**, form of use **VII.**

- **Olive oil,** its consumition to be anti-bacterial of anti-inflatatory propertierties protects against infections and promotes tissue healing. Keeping the inmune system strengthened, see **description of the Olive oil.**

- **Onion,** its consumption it has **antibacterial** and antifungal properties thanks to the phytochemicals that it possesses, see **description of plant.**

- **Orange,** the infusion ingested of its leaves is used **as antibacterial strengthens** the immune system and the purifying processes of the organism, see **description of the plant.**

- **Pansy,** the infusion is a solution against **the flu,** see **description of plant.**

- **Paronychia plant,** the infusion ingested it is used **to treat flu symptoms,** see **description of the plant.**

- **Parsley,** increase their consumption in autumn or winter, in broths and soups, thanks to their qualities **against the flu,** see **description of the plant.**

- **Patchouli,** inhalations relieve **flu symptoms,** see **description of plant.**

- **Peach,** its consumption **(moderate in children under 6 years),** for acute and infectious diseases, see **description of the plant.**

- **Perforate St John's-wort,** it acts as **an antibacterial,** as an **antibiotic. Encapsulated powder** can also be used, see **description of the plant,** form of use **VII (1).**

- **Pineapple,** beneficial as a detoxifying and purifying **food.** Also **drinking liquefaction** for its properties as a good **antibacterial,** see **description of the plant,** form of use **IX.**

- **Pollen,** endows the body with a **natural antibiotic,** as well as strength and stimulants, beneficial properties for children and young people, see **description of the Pollen,** form of consume **VIII (2 and 3).**

- **Pomegranate,** the consumption has **antibacterial** properties and effects for the body, see **description of the plant,** form of consume **VIII.**

- **Radish,** in **more than 3 years,** it is advisable to consume by its content of vitamin C and, the natural cleaning effects help to prevent viral infections by **doing antibiotic work,** see **description of the plant.**

- **Rye,** its consumption provides zinc and selenium, acting as **an antibacterial** and regulator of the immune system, see **description of the plant**, form of consume **VIII.**

- **Safflower,** the infusion ingested it is used **against the flu,** see **description of the plant.**

- **Salep drink,** its consumption it is traditionally used in the cold seasons **as a flu preventive,** see **description of the plant.**

- **Small-leaved lime,** the infusion ingested considered ideal **for flu-like symptoms.** Being diaphoretic is ideal **for fever** by controlling internal temperature by causing increased sweating, see **description of the plant.**

- **Soursop,** with the mixture of leaves and a handful of flowers you can make an infusion for **the flu,** see **description of the plant.**

- **Sowthistle,** the leaves in broth or as food are used as **antibacterial,** I feel useful as a purifier and depurative of the blood, see **description of the plant**, form of consume **VIII.**

- **Spearmint,** the infusion ingested, **from the age of 6 years,** it has a **great antibacterial power** and acts in a beneficial way in **the flu processes** see **description of the plant.**

- **Spirulina,** is used to increase and improve the immune system as **an antibacterial,** by having an effect on the activation of human lymphocytes, see **description of the plant.**

- **Strawberry plant,** depurative **antibacterial,** purifies the blood and removes waste from the organism, see **description plant**, form of use **VII.**

- **Sunflower,** consume regularly from seeds **as antibacterial,** increases the body's defenses, prevents and eradicates pathologies related to viruses, see **description of the plant.**

- **Tamarillo,** its consumption strengthens the immune system, **as an antibacterial** as well **as an antioxidant,** see **description of the plant.**

- **Tangerina,** the consumption for its vitamin C acts as **an antibacterial** and potentiates the immune system, see **description of the plant.**

- **Tea of Aragon,** the infusion is used for the **flu processes,** see **description of the plant.**

- **Watermelon,** its consumption it is very useful as **an antibiotic,** its properties strengthen the immune system by the presence of carotenoid substances. It **is restorative** for the amount of minerals being useful to combat fatigue and exhaustion, especially **and more frequently in summer,** see **description of the plant.**

- **West Indian cherry,** consume by immune stimulant **(antibacterial),** to strengthen the body's defenses and in prevention against **the flu,** see **description of the plant.**

- **Wheat,** its consumption used as **an antibacterial** is a source of protein, produces new cells and maintains the immune system, see **description of the plant.**

- **White clover,** the infusion ingested relieves **flulike processes,** see **description of the plant.**

Behavior problems - Nervousness - Poor sleep

Never replace the medication by the natural remedies. These remedies are supported, **you should always consult with your child's doctor.**

To avoid caries problems, when using ingested infusions, it is advisable, if necessary, to sweeten, use any sweetener that is indicated in the **Sweeteners** section.

Continue on next page

- **Banana,** for their vitamin B content, they are **very good for soothing** the nervous system, do not hesitate to eat bananas as a snack, see **description of the plant.**

- **Bitter lettuce,** very used the syrup to calm **the nerves** and provoke sleep, see **description of the plant.**

- **Calabash or Pumpkin,** its fruit is **the pumpkin,** its consumption it is **beneficial against insomnia,** see **description of the plant.**

- **Catnip,** the use of the infusion is used to exert a relaxing effect **that regulates sleep,** see **description of the plant.**

- **Chachacoma,** a tisane every night, **for insomnia** induces a restful and quiet sleep, see **description of the plant**, form of use **VII.**

- **Cherimoya,** as a tranquilizing sedative, it is very suitable for the treatment of **compulsive,** see **description of the plant.**

- **Cherry,** fruit that can be consumed without limit, contains melatonin, **helps to regulate sleep cycles,** see **description of the plant**.

- **Chickpea,** due to its high content of magnesium, phosphorus and B vitamins, it is suitable in situations **of lack of sleep or insomnia** and nervousness as **a sedative,** see **description of the plant.**

- **Cissampelos pareira,** using the infusion **as a sedative** is very useful in case of **mental disorders, epilepsy, delirium, convulsions,** see **description of the plant.**

- **Cowslip primrose,** the infusion ingested it is very useful **against** insomnia, see **description of the plant**, form of use **VII.**

- **Elms,** the infusion ingested it is used **as a sedative** to be a good soothing, see **description of the plant**, form of use **VII.**

- **Evening primrose,** the oil is used to treat problems of **hyperactivity in** children, see **description of the plant.**

- **Fennel,** the infusion in gargles of fennel, mint, sage and valerian herb, against the **blockade of the throat** causing **sleep apnea, insomnia** and hoarseness, see **description of the plant**, form of use **VII.**

- **Garden angelica,** the infusion of its leaves **for sleeping disorders and nervous alterations,** see **description of the plant.**

- **Grapevine,** the infusion of dried leaves ingested a dessert spoonful per cup of water for 10 minutes. Rest 10 more minutes and take every ¼ hour 1 tablespoon of this preparation **for insomnia.** The infusion of ingested dry leaves is used **as a sedative** in nervous states and **hyperexcitation, neurasthenia, neurosis,** see **description of the plant.**

- **Hops,** the infusion ingested (any way), it is beneficial to **fall asleep.** It stands out for **its relaxing and sedative action,** see **description of the plant**, form of use **VII.**

- **Indian pennywort,** the infusion ingested **for over 6 years** is very useful **in the lack of child care.** Also in disorders of child behavior and disorders such as: **hyper-excitability, hyperactive, impulsiveness, aggressiveness, litlle tolerance, etc.** It usually treat and is effective in improving neuronal dendritic growth and against Gilles de la Tourette syndrome, see **description of the plant.**

- **Large-leaved lime,** the infusion ingested favors the night rest, **helps to fall asleep,** reduces nervousness that prevents sleep. An infusion before bedtime is one of the most effective natural remedies **against insomnia.** Being a **mild sedative** can be used **as a soothing** nervous system, see **description of the plant.**

- **Lemon balm,** the infusion ingested being slightly **sedative,** combat **sleep disturbances,** it fights **nervous states, hyperactivity, irritability,** see **description of the plant.**

- **Lentil,** its consumption is convenient, iron deficiency can lead to develop **neurological problems** such as **attention deficit,** see **description of plant.**

- **Lettuce,** helps **calm** the nervous system, **and insomnia,** drinking a glass of juice helps us to **sleep better,** see **description of the plant.**

- **Linden tree,** before going to bed has **antispasmodic effects, acting against insomnia,** see **description of the plant,** form of use **VII.**

- **Martagon lily,** the infusion of flowers and bulbs, are effective **as a sedative** in diseases and **disorders of the nervous system,** see **description of the plant.**

- **Naranjilla,** it's effective in **promoting sleep,** see **description of plant.**

- **Narrow-leaf strap fern,** as drinking water on a regular basis combats **insomnia, and some nervous disorders,** see **description of the plant,** form of use **VII.**

- **Perforate St John's-wort,** the infusion ingested it acts **against insomnia. Encapsulated powder** can also be used, see **description of the plant,** form of use **VII (1).**

- **Potato,** its consumption it is convenient **against the insomnia when falling asleep,** see **description of the plant.**

- **Red pepper,** its consumption containing **vitamin B6 and magnesium, it reduces insomnia,** see **description of the plant.**

- **Rooibos,** the infusion ingested for its relaxing qualities it is beneficial **against nervousness relaxing our organism and our mind.** Being something sedative **helps to sleep better at night** because **it does not contain theine,** see **description of the plant.**

- **Saffron,** food supplement that, due to **its sedative** and aromatic substances, helps to combat anxiety and nervousness, see **description of the plant.**

- **Small-leaved lime,** the infusion ingested it is relaxing of the nervous system **induces sleep,** its action is mild, take 1 hour before only for isolated cases **of lack of sleep,** see **description of the plant.**

- **Soursop,** the chewed leaves have a high sedative power, it serves **as a sedative,** calms the nerves and acts against **the insomnia** to sleep better, see **description of the plant.**

- **Spearmint,** the infusion ingested, **from the age 6 years,** it is used for its **sedative properties** are ideal in **insomnia problems,** see **description plant.**

- **Spirulina**, of high content in melatonin in infusion or its consumption **is indicated for insomnia,** see **description of the plant.**

- **Tea of Aragon,** the infusion ingested it is an excellent **nervous toning,** as it does not contain theine, it has a **sedative and relaxing effect,** see description of the plant.

- **West Indian cherry,** fruit that regulates **sleep cycles or insomnia,** see description of the plant.

- **Wheat,** adequate intake of folic acid benefits and avoids **neural tube defects in sleeping children,** see **description of the plant.**

- **White horehound,** the infusion ingested it is used **as a sedative** for nervous disorders, see **description of the plant.**

- **Yam,** it serves **over 6 years,** to treat **insomnia,** see **description of plant.**

- **Yellow trumpetbush,** the infusion ingested it acts as a soothing **and intense sedative,** to relax the **nervous disorders,** see **description of plant.**

- **Finally,** we describe the plants that only **the simple infusion is necessary to ingest,** in this case to favor the night **rest helping to get to sleep** reducing the states of nervousness that prevent sleeping with the following plants:

Honeysuckle, Lemon verbena, Myrrh, Tansy, Valerian, Vanilla, Virginia water horehound.

If the infusion is going to be **used frequently,** its recommend **boiling the plant in a liter of water, or in the amount of water that we create** according to the daily use to be taken, thus way we will avoid time in its preparation and instead of the prepared bags that they sell you can buy in bulk to economize. It can **also be potentiated** with different plants for the same ailment, but it is convenient **to always remember** the perfect use of each plant used according **to its description,** in case there is any **interaction with drugs or possible contraindications.**

Burns - Sun rays

Never replace the medication by the natural remedies. These remedies are supported, **you should always consult with your child's doctor.**

- **Almond,** using grated almonds **on the burns,** cures, disinfects and relieves pain, see **description of the plant.**

- **Aloe vera,** relieves and prevents **blisters from oil, water or sunburn,** see **description of the plant.**

- **Apple,** the poultice of an apple mush is used for the treatment of **burns,** see **description of the plant.**

- **Beans,** in external use by poultices can be used against **burns,** to do this with a spoonful of dried pods cut from beans to 250 gr. of cold water, boil, the liquid and even the pods are used to make the compresses, see **description of the plant.**

- **Bloodroot,** topical infusion heals **burn wounds,** see **description of the plant**, form of use **VII.**

- **Breckland thyme,** the infusion is used by dressings or ointments, **in burns,** see **description of the plant.**

- **Broadleaf cattail,** the infusion through washes and dressings heals **the burns,** see **description of the plant.**

- **Cissampelos pareira,** the leaves cooked and crushed, **in plaster,** are used for **burns,** see **description of the plant.**

- **Clary sage,** the infusion or its oil in topical use, relieves and **heals the burns,** see **description of the plant.**

- **Cornstarch,** against **sunburn** that can cause very annoying injuries, being able to leave scars and cause skin irritations. To refresh the areas affected by UV rays, simply prepare a paste of cornstarch and water, and apply on the skin, see **description of the Corn and of the Cornstarch.**

- **Dyer's greenweed,** the infusion by washing or dressing heals and relieves **burns,** see **description of the plant.**

- **Echinacea,** it is enough to dilute 5 drops of its tincture in half a teaspoon (for dessert) of water and impregnate a dressing and apply directly on **the ampule,** see **description of the plant.**

- **Egg withe,** you can apply the clear on **the burned skin,** relieves and cure, see **description on Eggshell.**

- **Elms,** the infusion is used **in ointments, for burns,** see **description of the plant,** form of use **V.**

- **Escarole,** its consumption is recommended against situations **such as sun exposure** and environmental pollution, see **description of the plant.**

- **Geranium or Cranesbills,** the oil in topical use is used to relieve and heal **burns, see description of the plant**.

- **Honey,** can be applied on the skin to heal **burns, see description Honey.**

- **Horse chestnut,** the infusion of its leaves (without sweetening) and in topical use, **creams or ointments,** act as a **natural sunscreen,** while protecting, nourishing and softening by its high content in allantoin, it also serves **for normal burns.** They exist in specialized stores creams and ointments, see **description of the plant.**

- **Horsetail,** the poultice or the infusion in topical use is used for **burns,** relieving them, see **description of the plant**, form of use **IV.**

- **Ivy,** the infusion in topical use of the tender stems, boiled in a fatty medium, they are used **for sunburn,** see **description of the plant**.

- **Large-leaved lime,** the infusion in topical use results in immediate relief for the skin in case **of sunburn,** see **description of the plant.**

- **Lettuce,** in the **burns** apply apply or washing the lettuce juice in the burned area, when boiling the leaves for 15 minutes and strain, see **description of the plant.**

- **Marsh mallow,** the **root extracts** applied directly reduce **burns,** see **description of the plant.**

- **Martagon lily,** the leaves can be applied to the skin in order to reduce inflammation and swelling **of burns,** see **description of the plant.**

- **Myrrh,** the infusion or the oil in topical use helps **to heal and disinfect burns,** see **description of the plant.**

- **Olive oil,** in topical use apply on the skin to heal and relieve **burns,** see **description of the Olive oil.**

- **Papaya,** consumption **from 3 years,** due to its high content of beta-carotene, promotes and maintains the tan, and **prevents the appearance of sunburn,** see **description of the plant.**

- **Patchouli,** a small amount in topical use, diluted in another oil, serves to calm **the burns** (also in dressing), see **description of the plant.**

- **Perforate St John's-wort,** its oil in topical use is effective against burns, see **description of the plant.**

- **Pomegranate,** the oil its seed protects from the harmful effects of **the sun's ultraviolet rays,** that can cause wrinkles and increase the risk of skin cancer; apply one or two droplets spread by the skin clean and dry at least once a day, see **description of the plant**.

- **Potato,** its consumption is convenient for vitamin C, develops its ability to improve the texture of the skin and **to prevent the damage caused by the sun,** see **description of the plant.**

- **Pumpkin,** a poultice of well-washed and crushed leaves is used **for** burns, see **description of the plant.**

- **Rowan,** cooking and tincture in topical use is used **to heal burns,** see description of the plant.

- **Sanicle,** the infusion in washes or dressings **for burns,** see **description of the plant.**

- **Spearmint,** the infusion with **olive oil** is an excellent compress ointment to soothe and heal **burns,** see **description of the plant.**

- **Spirulina,** the beta-carotene it contains is useful **to protect the skin** from the sun's effect by stimulating the secretion of melanin, see description of the plant.

- **Tansy,** the infusion through washes and dressings heals **the burns,** see description of the plant.

- **Tomato,** the topical application of tomato juice, in the form of a plaster, is used to heal **wounds and burns.** Regular consumption of tomato protects the skin against UV rays, (**it is convenient to monitor the excess in the smallest**, being dual like constipation or diarrhea), see **description of the plant.**

- **Verdolaga,** the infusion in poultice or dressing, relieves and heals **the burns,** see **description of the plant.**

- **Water,** wash the skin with cold water using dressings **in the burns,** several times a day.

- **White horehound,** the infusion is used in topical use to relieve and **heal burns,** see **description of the plant.**

- **White nettle,** the infusion of flowers and flowery tips used in topical use by washing of washes or dressings, they heal and cool **the burns.** Also the tinctures in topical use, see **description of the plant**, form of use **VII.**

Control and problems of urine

Never replace the medication by the natural remedies. These remedies are supported, **you should always consult with your child's doctor**.

To avoid caries problems, when using ingested infusions, it is advisable, if necessary, to sweeten, use any sweetener that is indicated in the **Sweeteners** section.

- **Pansy,** the infusion ingested it is interesting **for the urinary system,** by contributing positively in the treatment of the annoying symptoms that cause **the difficult micturition,** see **description of the plant**.

- **Perforate St John's-wort,** the infusion **for enuresis** due to anxiety or nervous irritation in the bladder, especially in children, drink 2 cups daily (morning and night), see **description of the plant**, form of use **VII (1).**

- **Thyme,** the ingested infusion of boiling 50 grams of thyme in 1 liter of water for 10 minutes is used **against infantile enuresis, see description of the plant.**

Diarrhea - Gastroenteritis

Never replace the medication by the natural remedies. These remedies are supported, **you should always consult with your child's doctor**.

To avoid caries problems, when using ingested infusions, it is advisable, if necessary, to sweeten, use any sweetener that is indicated in the **Sweeteners** section.

- **Achiote tree,** against **diarrhea,** the infusion of 2 gr. of the shell that wraps the seed in 100 ml. of water, and take 3 times a day, see **description of the plant.**

- **Agrimony,** the infusion to counteract **diarrhea** is its best-known use, see **description of the plant**, form of use **VII.**

- **Ajuga iva,** the infusion as **anti diarrheic,** see **description of the plant.**

- **Apple,** the juice or directly consumed **is astringent** to fight **diarrhea,** see description of the plant.

- **Bighead/Conehead thyme,** the infusion ingested it is used **to** decrease and cut diarrhea, see **description of the plant.**

- **Bistort,** the infusion ingested for **diarrhea** for their astringent virtues, see **description of the plant**, form of use **VII.**

- **Black mulberry,** the infusion ingested of its leaves and the juice of the fruits is used **against diarrhea,** see **description of the plant.**

- **Bloodroot,** the infusion ingested it is perfect **to avoid diarrhea,** see **description of the plant,** form of use **VII.**

- **Breckland thyme,** the infusion ingested for **diarrhea,** see **description of the plant.**

- **Broadleaf cattail,** the infusion ingested it is used **for diarrhea** or dysentery, to regulate the stomach digestive system, see **description plant.**

- **Broadleaf plantain,** the infusion ingested it helps to heal problems such **as diarrhea,** see **description of the plant,** form of use **VII.**

- **Cecropia,** it is astringent and fights **diarrhea,** see **description of the plant,** form of use **VII.**

- **Cherry / Cherrys tree,** leaves or tails of the fruit **is effective against diarrhea,** see **description of the plant.**

- **Chestnut tree,** highlights its great power to combat **diarrhea,** see **description of the plant,** form of use **VII (1).**

- **Chilean myrtle,** for the **intestine** and against **dysentery,** see **description of the plant,** form of use **VII.**

- **Cissampelos pareira,** acts in **a dual way,** as **a laxative and purgative** in case of constipation, and **against dysentery,** see **description of plant.**

- **Common fleabane,** the infusion ingested it is effective, against dysentery, **intense diarrhea,** see **description of the plant.**

- **Coriander,** consumption relieves **diarrhea** caused by a microbial infection, see **description of the plant.**

- **Durmast oak,** the infusion ingested **3 or 4** times daily, relieves or **cuts diarrhea,** see **description of the plant,** form of use **VII.**

- **Eastern black walnut,** the infusion is used for its antispasmodic properties **as an antidiarrheal,** see **description of the plant.**

- **Elms,** the infusion ingested it is used against **diarrea,** see **description of the plant,** form of use **VII.**

- **Fennel,** la infusión ingerida of its leaves **or seeds,** relieves diarrhea, see **description of the plant,** form of use **VII.**

- **Geranium or Cranesbills,** the infusion ingested, in small doses, it is used **against diarrhea,** see **description of the plant.**

- **Gum arabic tree,** great astringent against **diarrhea,** see **description of the plant.**

- **Heath speedwell,** the infusion ingested being astringent is used **against diarrhea,** see **description of the plant.**

- **Herb Bennet,** the infusion as astringent tonic **fights diarrhea,** good stomach **tonic and gastrointestinal problems,** see **description of the plant,** form of use **VII (1).**

- **Honeysuckle,** the infusion ingested it is used effectively **in intestinal dysentery,** see **description of the plant,** form of use **VII.**

- **Hops,** the infusion ingested (any), is recommended to **treat diseases of the digestive and stomach system such as colitis,** see **description of the plant,** form of use **VII.**

- **Horsetail,** the infusion ingested it is used against **diarrhea,** see **description of the plant,** form of use **VII.**

- **Indian fig opuntia,** its consumption as an astringent helps to control **and stop diarrhea,** see **description of the plant.**

- **Jasmine,** drink jasmine tea as an aid in preventing diseases such **as** diarrhea, see **description of the plant.**

- **Kaki fruit,** the tannins of some varieties, and of **the kaki that have not fully matured,** they confer **astringent properties to treat diarrhea,** see **description of the plant.**

- **Kelp,** its consumption it is good to **cut the diarrhea,** due to alginic acid, see **description of the plant.**

- **Kinnikinnick,** the infusion ingested of its leaves is considered **a good anti diarreic,** sweeten to taste and drink, see **description of the plant.**

- **Kudzu,** consumption is **antidiarrheal,** but once the flora is regulated being **bipolar acting** makes it as a laxative, see **description of the plant.**

- **Lemon balm,** the infusion ingested it is **slightly astringent** and good **for tackle occasional diarrea,** see **description of the plant.**

- **Lemon verbena,** the infusion ingested helps control **diarrea,** see **description of the plant.**

- **Lilac,** the infusion ingested of bark or flowers to **treat diarrhea,** see **description of the plant.**

- **Loosestrife,** the infusion ingested it is ideal for **stopping and curing diarrhoea,** showing a great curative activity, especially when they carry a risk of dehydration, see **description of the plant.**

- **Marsh mallow,** the infusion ingested **of the leaves and roots** is used to **treat diarrhea,** see **description of the plant.**

- **Mountain everlasting,** you can cut **the diarrhea** with the infusion, see **description of the plant.**

- **Oregano,** the infusion ingested fights **diarrhoeal processes**, see **description of the plant,** form of use **VII.**

- **Perforate St John's-wort,** the infusion ingested acts against **diarrhea. Encapsulated powder** can also be used, see **description of the plant,** form of use **VII (1).**

- **Pomegranate,** the infusion ingested of the shell and bark of the tree is used **against diarrhea,** its consumption helps by its astringent property. Another remedy is the infusion with 30 gr. of flowers per liter of water, let stand for 15 minutes, sweeten and drink, see **description of the plant.**

- **Psoralea,** the infusion ingested fights **diarrhea,** see **description of the plant,** form of use **VII.**

- **Pumpkin,** the puree acts **against diarrhea,** boil 100 gr. of mature pulp in a liter of water, halved, crushed, and consumed, **the excess can have an opposite effect,** see **description of the plant.**

- **Quince,** its consumption it is very effective to treat **diarrhea,** see **description of the plant.**

- **Rice,** the liquid of its decoction used as day water, is very effective against **gastroenteritis, diarrhea,** see **description of the plant.**

- **Rooibos,** the infusion ingested, **it is advisable to watch over the smallest ones, given their dual property,** it can be an adequate traditional remedy **in case of diarrhea or constipation,** see **description of the plant.**

- **Rowan,** ingested cooking (including nuts), is used **against diarrhea,** see **description of the plant,** form of use **VII (1).**

- **Rye,** its contribution of fiber and mucilage favors the intestinal transit with easy evacuation, **in turn, being dual can act as anti-diarrheal,** see **description of the plant,** form of consume **VIII.**

- **Sage,** ingested can be used **from 6 years, never more than three daily infusions,** against **diarrhea,** see **description of the plant.**

- **Salep drink,** as an **antidiarrheal** it is very used in children, see **description of the plant.**

- **Sanicle,** the infusion ingested fights **dysentery** and intestinal parasites, see **description of the plant.**

- **Soursop,** is **anti-diarrheal** in cases of infection or eating disorders, see **description of the plant.**

- **Sowthistle,** the broth from the leaves is used to **treat diarrhea,** see **description of the plant,** form of consume **VIII.**

- **Spiked loosestrife,** the infusion is used mainly in the treatment of **infantile diarrhea with danger of dehydration** where it shows a surprising activity, **use with extreme caution,** see **description of the plant.**

- **Tamarind,** the infusion ingested helps to keep the body well hydrated in states of dehydration **and diarrhea,** see **description of the plant,** form of use **VII.**

- **Tea of Aragon,** the infusion ingested **can act in a dual way** against **diarrhea and as a laxative,** see **description of the plant.**

- **Thyme,** highly effective infusion to treat **diarrhea,** see **description plant.**

- **Tomato,** it is advisable to **monitor their consumption in the smallest,** having the dual faculty, to prevent **constipation and diarrhea,** see **description of the plant.**

- **Verdolaga,** is used **the juice in cases of diarrhea,** see **description plant.**

- **Walnut tree,** The infusion is used for its antispasmodic properties **as an antidiarrheal,** see **description of the plant,** form of use **VII.**

- **West Indian cherry,** being astringent, this fruit can be consumed for the treatment **of diarrhea,** see **description of the plant.**

- **White Chilean myrtle,** the infusion is excellent **against diarrhea,** also in enemas, see **description of the plant.**

- **White clover,** the infusion ingested acts as an **astringent against** diarrhea, see **description of the plant.**

- **White nettle,** the infusion of the flowers and flowery tips ingested, or cooked, act and cure **diarrhea,** see **description of the plant,** forms of use and consume **VII and VIII.**

Eye and ear problems

Never replace the medication by the natural remedies. These remedies are supported, **you should always consult with your child's doctor**.

To avoid caries problems, when using ingested infusions, it is advisable, if necessary, to sweeten, use any sweetener that is indicated in the **Sweeteners** section.

- **Ajuga iva,** the infusion in topical use to apply in the form of **washes or dressings,** for **conjunctivitis, blepharitis** (eyelids), see **description of plant.**

- **Apple,** in topical use by the poultice of an apple mush for the **inconvenience eyepieces** using it boiled and cold, if possible, apply at night, see **description of the plant.**

- **Bitter Lettuce,** for eye problems, infusions and decoctions of the leaves are used for **washing decongestants,** and in compresses, against **inflammations and irritations of the eyes,** see **description of the plant.**

- **Black mulberry,** the consumption of its fruits serves to slow down the progression of some **diseases of the vision, especially of degenerative type,** see **description of the plant.**

- **Broadleaf plantain,** the **distilled** infusion of this plant is widely used as an eye lotion, to treat **irritations, sinusitis, and eye infections,** see **description of the plant,** form of use **VII.**

- **Brussels sprout,** its high amount of vitamin C, as **an antioxidant** is beneficial for **hearing and** sight, see **description of the plant.**

- **Cantaloupe,** beneficial its consumption to contain carotenoids as lutein and zeaxanthin, necessary for **the good functioning of sight,** see **description of the plant.**

- **Carrot,** WHO considers vitamin A deficiency as the most important cause of **childhood blindness** in developing countries, see **description of plant.**

- **Clary sage,** in the Middle Ages it was called "clean-eyes", the term sclarea is derived from the Latin clarus, which means "clear" or "clean". The infusion in topical use **cleanses the eyes purifying** them of evils like the sight tired or the blurred, see **description of the plant.**

- **Chamomile,** the infusion ingested or in topical use in washing **for styes,** and as eye drops, also internally and externally, to reduce swellings such **as dark circles. In dressings, cold packs** or as eye drops **for sinusitis,** see **description of the plant.**

- **Chard,** its consumption it is beneficial for eye infections such **as conjunctivitis,** see **description of the plant.**

- **Cornflower,** being almost antibiotic in case **of conjunctivitis, bathe the eyes** with a few drops to relax them, see **description plant,** form of use **VII.**

- **Durmast oak,** for **conjunctivitis,** boil 1 tablespoon of rind washed in 1 cup of water 5 minutes. Rest and cool, wash several times a day. **The infusion** by compresses or dressings is used **for swollen eyes,** see **description of the plant,** form of use **VII.**

- **Eastern black walnut,** the infusion of the crust in topical use to wash **the eyes** in their affections, see **description of the plant.**

- **Echinacea,** effective for **annoying styes,** usingthe infusion in topical use, see **description of the plant.**

- **English primrose,** the infusion of **your flowers in topical use** is used **for ear conditions such as utricula.** Used on the eyes helps in the **blepharitis,** and relieves the annoying **conjunctivitis,** see **description plant.**

- **Garden nasturtium,** the infusion or decoction in rinses and dressings is quite effective **for styes,** see **description of the plant,** form of use **VII.**

- **Grapevine,** in ocular problems such as **conjunctivitis, blepharitis - styes, sap is used in topical use,** it is considered one of the most important natural eye drops and very suitable in ocular treatments, cleans the eye and improves the vision of the affected person. In the **inflammations of the conjunctive**, the application of vine shoot water will help to reduce inflammation **and cure itching or pain.** Apply a fresh drop from the plant in the form of eye drops. **The liquid can not be stored,** it is damaged, it must be applied immediately, see **description of the plant.**

- **Green pepper,** its consumption it is beneficial to **the health of the ear.** It also helps to have **better vision,** see **description of the plant.**

- **Gum arabic tree,** its astringent properties to wash eyes, are very effective for cases of **infections or inflammations** of the eye conjunctiva, is one of the most natural remedies used to treat naturally the cases **of conjunctivitis,** so common in young children, see **description of the plant.**

- **Helychrysum,** it is used for **conjunctivitis,** the infusion in **topical use,** see **description of the plant.**

- **Horsetail,** the infusion by **washing or dressing** is used **against conjunctivitis,** see **description of the plant,** form of use **VII.**

- **Jew's ear,** its consumption it is beneficial **against eye inflammations,** see **description of the plant.**

- **Kale,** the consumption by the presence of contained vitamin A, is good **for the vision,** see **description of the plant.**

- **Kinnikinnick,** the infusion **of its leaves** is used by means of washes or dressings, without sweetening, to combat **eye inflammations,** see **description of the plant.**

- **Kiwi,** it should be consumed by its **beneficial properties for vision,** see **description of the plant.**

- **Lettuce,** improves **conjunctivitis** problems by preparing a juice and apply in washes or dressings, see **description of the plant.**

- **Mallow,** the infusion used as **eye drops** is used for cases of **dryness or irritation of the eyes,** see **description of the plant.**

- **Myrtle,** the infusion ingested or oil in topical use **(in older than 6 years),** act against otitis, see **description of the plant,** forms of use **VI and VII.**

- **Nectarine,** essential nutrient because it **develops good vision,** see **description of the plant.**

- **Niaouli,** is usually used in topical use **for infections such as otitis,** see **description of the plant.**

- **Olive,** the infusion of the leaves, ingested, acts against the **tinnitus in the ears,** see **description of the plant.**

- **Oregano,** the infusion **in topical use** it is used **against otitis.** The infusion **ingested** it is beneficial t**o the eyes,** see **description plant,** form of use **IV.**

- **Pansy,** in topical use as washes or dressings, is used **for conjunctivitis, corneal conditions, blepharitis,** see **description of the plant.**

- **Papaya,** consumption **from 3 years, to prevent vitamin A** deficiency, cause of **childhood blindness,** in developing tropical and subtropical countries, see **description of the plant.**

- **Quince,** in **eye problems** it is very useful to apply the pulp to the affected area with pain. Also with the seeds, preparing a cooking and use as a lotion or poultice with 2 tablespoons of seeds in 1 liter of water, see **description of the plant.**

- **Red cabbage,** antioxidant very good consumption for your benefit **to the eye,** see **description of the plant.**

- **Saturn peaches,** its consumption to be rich in carotenes and vitamins C, A, B1, B2, B6 and minerals as potassium, phosphorus, magnesium, sulfur, iron and calcium, they all **protect the eyesight,** see **description of plant.**

- **Spiked loosestrife,** the infusion ingested it is beneficial **for the eye** contains antitumoral substances and anthocyanin among its active ingredients, **capable of improving some vision problems.** In topical use by washing it can be beneficial **in case of conjunctivitis,** perfectly filter the liquid before use, see **description of the plant.**

- **Tamarillo,** its consumption serves to strengthen **the visión,** see **description of the plant.**

- **Verdolaga,** the infusion using poultice or dressing is used to relieve **conjunctivitis.** Good remedy for the **ocular inflammations,** see **description of the plant.**

- **Walnut tree,** the infusion of its leaves in washes or dressings, **for ocular inflammations,** see **description of the plant,** form of use **VII.**

- **Water,** cold water compresses, whenever possible, and at night, **for swollen eyelids.**

- **White clover,** the infusion in topical use, by washing or dressing against **conjunctivitis.** For any **ocular inflammation,** see **description of the plant.**

- **White nettle,** for **the ears, in topical use** to use the hot steam of the decoction, see **description of the plant.**

Fevers - Throat

Never replace the medication by the natural remedies. These remedies are supported, **you should always consult with your child's doctor.**

To avoid caries problems, when using ingested infusions, it is advisable, if necessary, to sweeten, use any sweetener that is indicated in the **Sweeteners** section.

- **Achiote tree,** in **throat inflammations,** the infusion with a bunch of achiote herbs and a tablespoon for dessert of ginger plant, boiled in a liter of water, rinse every 8 h. as minimum, see **description of the plant.**

- **Agrimony,** in rinses or gargles helps the healing **of throat inflammations,** see **description of the plant,** form of use **VII.**

- **Ajuga iva,** against **pharyngitis, without sweetening,** see **description of the plant.**

- **Apple,** its consumption it's good help **against fever,** see **description of the plant.**

- **Ash,** the infusion ingested as an antipyretic, it **lowers fever** and as a remedy against **the flu**, see **description of the plant.**

- **Beet,** gargle **in throat** conditions such **as tonsillitis,** it is convenient to scratch and mix with a tablespoon of vinegar, liquefy until all the juice is released, see **description of the plant.**

- **Bergamot orange,** appreciated antipyretic **against fever** for malaria. The diluted oil applied through **inhalations, gargles and massages** will obtain a quick recovery in **the throat,** see **description of the plant.**

- **Bistort,** the infusion and liquefaction by their demulcent virtues favor **the throat, laryngitis (aphonia) and pharyngitis** when gargle with the infusions, see **description of the plant,** forms of use **VII and IX.**

- **Bitter lettuce,** very used syrup against sore **throats, pharyngitis,** see **description of the plant.**

- **Black mulberry / Blackberry,** the juice of its fruits is a **refreshing** and invigorating drink that helps **in case of fever.** The infusion of its leaves acts against the discomforts of the **throat, tonsils, larynx.** Also **in gargles,** see **description of the plant,** form of consumption **VIII.**

- **Black mustard,** its consumption **against fever** it acts as a febrifuge, taking from 5 to 6 whole grains of black mustard, dissolved in a cup of water. Its consumption or in gargles helps in the **affections of the throat,** see **description of the plant.**

- **Black pepper,** the infusion ingested, (without excess) is used **to lower fever,** see **description of the plant.**

- **Bloodroot,** the infusion ingested it is used for discomfort of **the throat,** also in gargles, see **description of the plant,** form of use **VII.**

- **Breckland thyme,** the infusion ingested or in gargles and rinses, is used in **throat conditions** and for **pharyngitis,** see **description of the plant.**

- **Broadleaf plantain,** the infusion ingested and in gargles is good for **throat problems**, laryngitis, pharyngitis, **aphonia. Ingested is very used** to **lower fever,** see **description of the plant,** form of use **VII.**

- **Calamus,** the infusion or liquefaction ingested, **used from 3 years,** is good sudorific helping to **fight fever,** see **description of the plant,** forms of use **VII and IX.**

- **Cantaloupe,** the juice of its pulp is used to **lower the fever,** see **description of the plant.**

- **Catnip,** the infusion is used to lower **fevers.** Also in the affections **of the throat** (nasal and pharyngeal), in tonsillitis (through poultices in the neck), see **description of the plant.**

- **Cecropia,** acts against fever, and to solve **throat problems such as tonsils,** see **description of the plant,** form of use **VII.**

- **Chachacoma,** excellent to fight whooping cough in syrup, **consult the doctor or specialist the form of use.** Relief is usually feels after the third day of treatment, see **description of the plant.**

- **Chamomile,** the infusion in gargle for **the throat** is used against their discomforts in general. Also the gargles of **chamomile infusion with:** sage, relieves sore **throats and tonsillitis,** see **description of the plant.**

- **Chestnut tree,** is used against inflammations of the **throat, tonsils, pharyngitis, and laryngitis,** the cause of **aphonia,** see **description of the plant,** forms of use **VII (1 and 3).**

- **Chilean myrtle,** the decoction of crust and leaves is used. Also the cooking of the roots for **throat,** laundry and gargle problems, two or three times a day, see **description of the plant,** form of use **VII.**

- **Cinnamon,** the infusion is very useful to balance the body temperature, so it **reduces fever.** It is used **for sore throats** to improve tonsils, pharyngitis and laryngitis (also in gargles), see **description of the plant.**

- **Cinnamon with honey,** combat and relieve **throat conditions (from 1 year),** mixing a tablespoon with warm water and taking sips while gargling, see **description of the plant and of the Honey.**

- **Cissampelos pareira,** the infusion ingested it is useful in case of **typhoid fevers,** see **description of the plant.**

- **Clary sage,** the ingested infusion for the **sore throat.** Against throat pains and affections such as **tonsillitis,** irritation of **laryngitis, aphonia and hoarseness,** also by compresses, see **description plant,** form of use **VII (4).**

- **Cornflower,** helps to **reduce fever** in cases of infections combines its antibiotic properties with the anti-inflammatory and **...Continue**

... antipyretics, **rich in mucilage,** tannins, flavonoids, abundant coloring pigments and mineral salts, see **description of the plant,** form of use **VII.**

- **Durmast oak,** for **throat conditions** as an antiseptic combat **pharyngitis, tonsillitis and laryngitis** when it affects **aphonia or hoarseness.** Make an infusion by pouring 2 tablespoons of washed crust into a cup of boiling water. Rest, cool, filter and gargle several times a day, see **description of the plant.**

- **Eastern black walnut,** the infusion of the ingested crust **to treat diphtheria in the throat.** In **gargling** it is effective **against aphonia and hoarseness.** Good for treating **fever types such as malaria,** see **description of the plant.**

- **Elder,** the infusion ingested and in gargles (witoout weetened) for sore **throat and tonsillitis,** see **description of the plant.**

- **Elms,** the infusion ingested it is used **against typhoid fevers,** see **description of the plant,** form of use **VII.**

- **Erythraea chilensis,** it is used as an **antiinflammatory** and sudorific **to cut intermittent fever,** and helps in convalescence, see **description of the plant,** form of use **VII.**

- **Fennel,** against **blockade of the throat** causing sleep apnea, insomnia and hoarseness, against **blockade of the throat** causing **sleep apnea, insomnia and hoarseness,** see **description of the plant,** form of use **VII.**

- **Fig,** for **throat inflammation** should boil for ¼ hour 20 gr. of dried figs to bits. Add a spoonful of honey **(in older than 1 year),** filter and rinse with the hot liquid. Another option is its cooking in milk for gargles, see **description of the plant and of the Honey.**

- **Geranium or Cranesbills,** the infusion ingested and in gargles, against sore **throat or tonsillitis,** see **description of the plant,** form of use **VII.**

- **Green pepper,** the broth of **his cooking by gargling, in the affections** of the throat cures pharyngitis, see **description of the plant.**

- **Gum arabic tree,** in gargling for **throat** infections, see **description of the plant.**

- **Hazel,** relieves **the fever,** see **description of the plant,** form of use **VII.**

- **Heath speedwell,** the infusion in gargles its used against **throat** irritation, **tonsillitis, laryngitis, pharyngitis,** see **description of the plant.**

- **Herb Bennet** it is used **in gargles and drink** for **throat** inflammations by **pharyngitis, tonsils or laryngitis, aphonia.** Against hot flashes **and fever,** see **description of the plant,** form of use **VII (2).**

- **Honeysuckle,** the infusion ingested and in gargles, it is successfully used **as an antiinflammatory for the throat,** laryngeal and pharyngeal conditions, internal infections, **aphonia.** The infusion of **the crust** is effective against **inflammation of the lymph nodes and mumps,** see **description of the plant,** form of use **VII.**

- **Horsetail,** the infusion in **rinses and gargle** fights **inflammations in the throat,** see **description of the plant,** form of use **VII.**

- **Iceland moss,** the double decoction ingested by the assembled components is particularly **indicated for throat discomfort,** in laryngitis, pharyngitis, causing **aphonias and hoarseness,** you can drink three cups a day, see **description of the plant,** form of use **VII.**

- **Jew's ear,** its consumption helps to heal **swollen and irritated throats** and is ideal for treating **tonsillitis,** see **description of the plant.**

- **Kudzu,** its consumption helps to reduce fever in the processes **related to colds, and coughs,** see **description of the plant.**

- **Large-leaved lime,** the infusion ingested it is an antipyretic that is used for **cases of mild fever,** see **description of the plant.**

- **Lemon,** its consumption with honey **(in more than 1 year)** or water, softens and improves **the throat affections,** see **description of the plant.**

- **Lemon balm,** the infusion ingested help to reduce cases **of fever,** see **description of the plant.**

- **Lemon grass,** the infusion ingested, **use the bags already made,** has **febrifuge** properties, see **description of the plant.**

- **Lilac,** the infusion ingested of the crust or flowers against **fever and hyperthermia,** in **throat problems, aphonia, hoarseness,** see **description of the plant.**

- **Loosestrife,** the infusion ingested or in rinses is very useful in **the throat** to treat and **heal pharyngitis,** see **description of the plant.**

- **Lungwort,** effective in cases of **inflammations of the throat and larynx.** It is recommended to drink 3 or 4 cups of hot decoction daily, and also gargle with the same amount of cooking, but lukewarm, see **description of the plant,** form of use **VII.**

- **Mallow,** the infusion **ingested or in gargles** is very effective **in throat problems** such as **tonsils,** pharyngitis, **aphonia, hoarseness,** wheezing, see **description of the plant.**

- **Mexican pepperleaf,** the infusion helps to lower **fever.** Also ingested or in topical use acts on **throat** conditions such as **laryngitis,** which could cause **hoarseness and aphonias** (in gargles), see **description of the plant.**

- **Mint,** see in **Fennel** form of use **VII.**

- **Mountain everlasting,** the infusion ingested to **lower the fever,** sweeten to taste. In **gargle** it improves the **...Continue on next page**

... inflammations of **throat, aphonia, tonsillitis, pharyngitis (without sweetening),** see **description of the plant.**

- **Myrrh,** the infusion **ingested and in gargles** is extremely useful **for throat** help in case of **pharyngitis, laryngitis,** see **description of the plant.**

- **Myrtle,** the infusion in gargles **(in older than 6 year),** combats **throat problems,** such **as laryngitis, aphonia or hoarseness,** see **description of the plant,** form of use **VII.**

- **Olive,** the infusion ingested **of leaves and crust** serves **to lower fever,** see **description of the plant.**

- **Oregano,** the infusion **ingested** it fights **pharyngitis and tonsillitis** in throat ailments, also in gargles, **without sweetening,** see **description of the plant,** form of use **VII.**

- **Pansy,** la infusión it is used in **sore throats** such as pain and **pharyngitis** (also in gargles), see **description of the plant.**

- **Paronychia plant,** the infusion ingested or in topical use to **lower the fever,** see **description of the plant.**

- **Patchouli,** in topical use, diluted in other oil **helps** fight **fever**-causing infections and **reduces corporal temperature,** through massage, see **description of the plant.**

- **Perforate St John's-wort,** the infusion ingested or in gargles is used **for throat infections. Encapsulated powder** can also be used, see **description of the plant,** form of use **VII (1).**

- **Prunus,** the infusion of the crust to be astringent **removes fever,** see **description of the plant.**

- **Quince,** for **throat problems** in conditions and inflammations the infusion is used to gargle, you should cook 2 or 3 quinces **... Continue**

... with skin and seeds. Strain and extract the juice, rest a few days to mix it with 1 glass of warm water and use, see **description of the plant.**

- **Radish,** in **older than 3 years, clear the sinuses** and calm **the sore throat,** see **description of the plant.**

- **Raisin,** its consumption it has **germicidal properties,** it is used a lot to **lower fever,** see **description of the plant.**

- **Rice,** the water resulting from the decoction of rice is beneficial **in the febrile processes,** from babies, see **description of the plant.**

- **Safflower,** serves as diaphoretic, a hot tea produces a profuse perspiration inducing the same at a drop in temperature body **(lowers fever),** and **all febrile illnesses.** Also in the treatment **of measles,** see **description of the plant.**

- **Saffron,** drink a cup of infusion with 0.5 gr. in 250 ml of boiling water, it is a good remedy. Powerful diaphoretic, that is, that favors sweating, being **ideal for fever pictures,** see **description of the plant.**

- **Sage,** against **sore throats** can be used ingested **(from 6 years),** but **never more than three daily infusions. It also** relieves **sore throats and tonsillitis** gargles of sage with chamomile. Another option to see **in Fennel,** see **the different descriptions of the plants.**

- **Sanicle,** the infusion in **gargles or rinses** fights **throat affections** is used in cases of **pharyngitis, tonsillitis, laryngitis, and aphonia,** see **description of the plant.**

- **Small-leaved lime,** the infusion due to its **diaphoretic property**, it is ideal **for fever** when controlling the internal temperature of the organism, and cause an increase in sweating, see **description of the plant.**

- **Sowthistle,** the broth of the **leaves and roots** can reduce **fever,** see **description of the plant,** form of consume **VIII.**

- **Spiked loosestrife,** the infusion ingested **(with caution)** or in gargles for sore **throat and pharyngitis,** see **description of the plant.**

- **Spiny restharrow,** it is used **for throat problems** such as tonsillitis (in gargle in a temperate form), see **description of the plant,** form of use **VII.**

- **Strawberry plant,** the infusion ingested of its leaves and roots is used **for the throat** in pharyngitis and stomatitis, making rinses or gargles, **without sweetening,** see **description of the plant,** form of use **VII.**

- **Sugarcane,** ideal for **febrile disorders** that can lead to seizures and protein loss in the body, helping to compensate for these protein losses **and recovery,** see **description of the plant,** form of use **IX.**

- **Tamarind,** the infusion ingested it is used **to fight bilious and inflammatory fevers**, for malarias, see **description plant,** form of use **VII.**

- **Tansy,** the infusion ingested acts against **the fever** to be sudorific, febrifuge (fever sender), see **description of the plant.**

- **Thyme,** the infusion ingested or in gargles fights sore **throat, laryngitis, pharyngitis, tonsillitis,** see **description of the plant.**

- **Valerian,** the infusion in gargles of fennel, mint, sage **(from 6 years),** and valerian, against **throat blockage** causing sleep apnea, **insomnia and hoarseness,** see **the different descriptions of the plants.**

- **Vanilla,** the infusion ingested help lower **fever,** see **description of plant.**

- **Virginia water horehound,** the infusion ingested it is commonly used to relieve **sore throat,** see **description of the plant.**

- **White clover,** the infusion ingested its used to **inflammation** in general, but also glandular, **prevents mumps.** Fights **the fever,** see **description of the plant.**

- **White mustard,** its consumption and in gargles helps in the affections of **the throat** such **as tonsillitis,** see **description of the plant.**

- **White nettle,** the infusion of **the root, ingested or in gargle,** for inflammations of the **throat, pharyngitis.** Also the **tincture in external topical use,** see **description of the plant.**

- **White pepper,** consume **(only cooked in powder),** to lower the **fever,** see **description of the plant.**

- **Yellow trumpetbush,** the infusion ingested **lowers fever** or fever symptoms, see **description of the plant.**

Growth/Development - Dentures - Bones

Never replace the medication by the natural remedies. These remedies are supported, **you should always consult with your child's doctor.**

To avoid caries problems, when using ingested infusions, it is advisable, if necessary, to sweeten, use any sweetener that is indicated in the **Sweeteners** section.

- **Agar Agar,** food that contains the necessary calcium to **favor the correct formation of bones and** teeth during periods **of growth,** see **description of the plant.**

- **Azuki red beans,** for its contribution of magnesium, potassium, phosphorus and calcium promotes **bone remineralization,** see **description of the plant.**

- **Banana,** consume banana and orange (natural or juice) **in the first two years of life** of babies can reduce the risk in the development of leukemia. Studies indicate that **eating at least** one banana a day reduces the probability of developing **asthma** by 34%. Also beneficial for the protection and conservation of **bone density,** see **the different descriptions of plants.**

- **Beans,** its consumption it is highly recommended if we want to **keep strong and healthy bones,** see **description of the plant.**

- **Cantaloupe,** in the smallest, its consumption is beneficial because it contains the micronutrients necessary **for growth,** in **bone** formation and effective **for dental,** see **description of the plant.**

- **Carob tree,** strengthens **teeth and bones,** its consumption **for the period of growth** infantile provides carbohydrates, vitamins A, B, C, E, minerals such as potassium, magnesium, iron, phosphorus, zinc, calcium, selenium, iodine, fatty acids, carotenoids, vegetable proteins and fiber, see **description of the plant.**

- **Catnip,** the infusion ingested its used to treat **muscle pain, and cold joints,** see **description of the plant.**

- **Chard,** very indicated in all the **development and infantile deficiencies** for the formation of collagen **in bones and teeth,** see **description of plant.**

- **Cherimoya,** in pediatrics it has dietary applications (in the form of purees or juices) due to its mineral content (calcium, phosphorus, iron), vitamins (group B, C, A), with proteins and sugars very **...Continue**

... advisable **in epoch of growth,** its content in vitamin C intervenes in the formation of collagen in **bones, teeth,** see **description of the plant.**

- **Cissampelos pareira,** the infusion in mouthwashes, **without sweetening,** it is used as an analgesic and antispasmodic for **dental and toothache pains,** see **description of the plant.**

- **Clementina,** for the **strengthening of bones, cartilages.** Perfect complement for **physical and muscular efforts,** after doing sports helps to rehydrate by the amount of water, see **description of the plant.**

- **Coconut,** fruit very rich in iron and potassium, mineral salts that participate in the own **mineralization of bones,** such as calcium, phosphorus or magnesium, see **description of the plant.**

- **Escarole,** the folate requirements are higher in children, therefore, including green leafy vegetables in their usual diet is a way valid to **prevent deficiencies**. The lack of this vitamin has also been related to **alterations in growth,** see **description of the plant.**

- **Geranium,** its used to the oil in topical use to relieve **joint pain,** see **description of the plant.**

- **Gladiolus,** its **fresh** rhizome is used to **reduce inflammation and relieve gum pain in the children during teething,** see **description of the plant.**

- **Grapefruit,** consume being rich in vitamin C, it helps to **preserve bone density,** see **description of the plant.**

- **Green pepper,** its consumption, by folates, it is necessary in the stage **of growth** of children in their diet, it is a good way to prevent deficiencies, and in the **formation of teeth.** For phosphorus, calcium and magnesium, they are important in **the formation of bone** and against **bone tuberculosis,** see **description of the plant.**

- **Grenadia,** one of the first foods that is recommended to integrate a baby **for growth,** for its many properties, being an excellent source of potassium, calcium, phosphorus and iron, see **description of the plant.**

- **Hazelnut,** it serves to strengthen and benefit the **joints and bones,** by its magnesium is able to strengthen the skeleton, storing and using in case of shortage, see **description of the plant.**

- **Hops,** the infusion ingested (any), having aperitive and antiseptic properties, useful to **stimulate the appetite** in inappetent, see **description of the plant,** form of use **VII.**

- **Kale,** its vitamin K gives properties to promote **bone health** by helping to fix calcium in them, see **description of the plant.**

- **Kiwi,** its consumption for providing vitamin C is especially recommended for periods **of child growth,** see **description of the plant.**

- **Lamb´s lettuce,** its consumption strengthens **the bones** and the growth of **the teeth** by its calcium content, see **description of the plant.**

- **Lentil,** is convenient to consume, iron deficiency can lead to develop **neurological problems** such as **attention deficit,** see **description of plant.**

- **Marjoram** the **essential oil** in alcoholic solution and external use, to perform **frictions in the affected joints,** see **description of the plant.**

- **Marsh mallow,** the roots applied gently are given **to infants in the first dentition** to reduce irritation, see **description of the plant.**

- **Naranjilla,** its consumption it is **highly recommended in children's diet** because it acts directly on the **formation of bones, teeth and tissues,** see **description of the plant.**

- **Nectarine,** its consumption it is good to **keep teeth healthy**. It is important in the function of transmitting and generating the nerve impulse **for muscle activity** to be rich in potassium, see **description of the plant.**

- **Olive oil,** its large amount of oleates promotes **calcification and bone mineralization,** see **description of the plant.**

- **Orange,** its consumption and the juice serve to preserve the **density of the bones,** see **description of the plant.**

- **Oregano,** the infusion **in topical use or the poultice** is used in **joints and bones** for **osteoarticular pain or inflammation.** It also eliminates **pain** and helps to **recover external injuries,** see **description of the plant,** forms of use **IV and VII.**

- **Papaya,** consume **from 3 years,** provides **chemo papain,** useful for **bones and treatment of herniated discs,** see **description of the plant.**

- **Passion fruit,** its consumption intervenes in the formation of collagen, beneficial for **the dental strengthening** and collaborates to **strengthen the bones** of the body, for its vitamin C, see **description of the plant.**

- **Pea,** food with an important source of calcium, essential for **teething and bones,** see **description of the plant.**

- **Peanut,** beneficial in the stage of **development and growth of children,** being very rich in proteins and good amino acids for the growth and development of the body, see **description of the plant.**

- **Pomegranate,** its consumption strengthens **the bones,** see **description of the plant,** form of consume **VIII.**

- **Potato,** its consumption it is convenient to contain **choline,** very important and versatile nutrient that in **physical efforts** helps **muscle movement,** containing iron, phosphorus, calcium, magnesium and zinc, contributes to the correct formation and **maintenance of bone structure,** see **description of the plant.**

- **Quinine,** in infusion, **non-alcoholic,** is effective to treat problems **such as rickets,** see **description of the plant.**

- **Radish,** in **older than 3 years,** regenerates **or increases** the formation of collagen **strengthening the bones.** The leaves are a great source of calcium, in addition to vitamins A, C and K, phosphorus, magnesium, iron, folic acid and fiber, raw, in tortilla, salads, in juices with other vegetables, see **description of the plant.**

- **Raisin grape,** is a **rich source of calcium,** its consumption serves to fortify the **bones and teeth,** providing the organism 40 mg. of calcium every 100 grams, see **description of the plant.**

- **Red cabbage,** one of the best vegetables that contributes **to bone growth** and mineral density. **Protects** against bone disease, see **description of the plant.**

- **Roquet,** beneficial to consume when containing vitamin K, it favors that the organism assimilates the calcium, beneficial **for the bones,** see **description of the plant.**

- **Saturn peaches,** the consumption of this fruit helps to **protect the state of the teeth,** see **description of the plant.**

- **Spinach,** its consumption it is beneficial for **the development of children,** because of its folic acid content (B9). Vegetable with high content of calcium and vitamin K, to **maintain bone health,** see **description plant.**

- **Thyme,** the infusion ingested relieves **bone pain,** see **description plant.**

- **Tomato,** its consumption helps for the maintenance of **teeth** and the maintenance of **healthy bones,** see **description of the plant.**

- **Turnip,** the consumption **of its leaves** are a great source of calcium, in addition to vitamins A, C and K, phosphorus, magnesium, iron, folic acid and fiber. Very good and useful when it comes to strengthening, regenerating or increasing collagen formation **for care of our bones.** They can be eaten raw, in tortilla, in salads, even in juices with other vegetables, see **description of the plant.**

- **Walnut tree,** the infusion ingested of its leaves fights **rickets,** see **description of the plant,** form of use **VII.**

- **Watermelon,** the consumption, for its properties, improves **the health of the bones.** Drinking watermelon juice before intense physical activity **helps reduce muscle pain the next day,** see **description of the plant.**

- **Wheat,** its consumption it is important and beneficial, because of its phosphorus, **for bone health,** see **description of the plant.**

- **White pepper,** its consumption **(only cooked in powder),** it is an excellent **source** of manganese, good **for bones,** see **description of plant.**

- Yellow pepper, its consumption regular helps maintain the **health of teeth and bones,** see **description of the plant.**

Hiccup

Never replace the medication by the natural remedies. These remedies are supported, **you should always consult with your child's doctor.**

To avoid caries problems, when using ingested infusions, it is advisable, if necessary, to sweeten, use any sweetener that is indicated in the **Sweeteners** section.

- Cardamom, boil ½ teaspoon fresh cardamom powder in 2 cups water, strain and drink, **older than 6 years,** a glass of this warm water to stop **hiccups,** see **description of the plant.**

- Lemon balm, the infusion ingested it is usually **effective against hiccups** by adding a pinch of mint and another of lemon balm, sweetened with honey **(from 1 year),** see **the different descriptions of the plants and of the Honey.**

- Mint, the infusion of mint alone is good **for hiccups.** You can **also combine** see in **Lemon balm.** Another option **in older than 6 years** to see in **Southern wormwood,** see **the different descriptions of the plants.**

- Southern wormwood, the infusion with a pinch of mint and another of southern wormwood, sweetened with honey, **for over 6 years,** it is usually effective against hiccups, see **the different descriptions of the plants and of the Honey.**

- Sugarcane, the water **with sugar cane** (preferably) is usually very effective against **hiccups** by relaxing the muscle of the diaphragm, see **description of the plant.**

- **Water,** with sugar cane (preferably) is usually very effective against hiccups by relaxing the muscle of the diaphragm. **In the form of ice,** keeping a piece (wrapped in cloth) for one minute next to the Adam's apple, is usually an alternative against hiccups.

- **White mustard,** against **hiccups,** being one of the most effective home remedies, mix ½ teaspoon of dessert with mustard seeds and ½ teaspoon dessert with pure butter and swallow the mixture. The hiccup will stop quickly, see **description of the plant.**

Intestines - Laxatives - Worms

Never replace the medication by the natural remedies. These remedies are supported, **you should always consult with your child's doctor**.

To avoid caries problems, when using ingested infusions, it is advisable, if necessary, to sweeten, use any sweetener that is indicated in the **Sweeteners** section.

- **Acorn,** as food is beneficial to the **intestine,** see **description of plant.**

- **Agar Agar,** of easy digestion, suitable for children and in patients. Regulates **intestinal transit** smoothly, without the irritating effects **associated with laxatives,** being a very rich fiber food, see **description of the plant.**

- **Almond,** acts effectively **as a laxative** given on an empty stomach **to a child,** see **description of the plant,** form of use **VI.**

- **Aloe vera,** ingestion of its inner gel or pulp (there are preparations) **has a laxative effect,** see **description of the plant.**

- **Amaranth,** it is used for constipation **as a laxative,** see **description of the plant,** form of consume **VIII.**

- **Asafoetida,** fights **irritable bowel** syndrome **(IBS).** Excellent **laxative,** prevents constipation. It acts against **worms,** see **description of the plant.**

- **Ash,** the infusion ingested its used to against **intestinal parasites and worms** and as **a laxative** for constipation, see **description of the plant.**

- **Azuki red beans,** promotes the growth of a **healthy intestinal flora,** regulating intestinal transit **as a laxative** improving constipation, see **description of the plant.**

- **Baccharises,** as a tonic helps to eliminate **intestinal parasites and worms,** see **description of the plant,** form of use **VII (1).**

- **Banana,** very rich in fiber, **consumed in moderation** is recommended for those who suffer from constipation by stimulating bowel movement **without the need to use laxatives,** see **description of the plant.**

- **Baobab tree,** very beneficial for the **intestinal flora,** see **description of the plant.**

- **Barley,** it is used **as a laxative** and **as day water**, it is good for its alkalizing power the content of vitamins and minerals, especially in convalescence. You can add barley semolina to your porridge, raw sometimes rejected by children under 1 year, better boil until it softens and mix, see **description of the plant,** form of use **VII.**

- **Bay laurel,** the infusion ingested relieves **stomach discomfort,** reducing **intestinal spasms,** see **description of the plant.**

- **Beet,** good **for bowel** work. **As a laxative** eat cooked with skin **and drink the liquid of the decoction,** see **description of the plant.**

- **Bergamot orange,** the fruit, the infusion and the diluted oil used for the process of expulsion of **intestinal worms,** see **description of the plant.**

- **Bitter-wood,** as a vermifuge in the form of an enema, **it eliminates pinworms, worms and parasites** that are usually ...**Continue on next page**

... located in the rectum and anus, where the effect of medications taken orally does not usually reach, see **description of plant,** form of use **IX.**

- **Black sesame,** very **rich in magnesium,** normalizes the **functioning of the intestine,** eliminates toxins and exerts a **laxative effect,** see **description of the plant.**

- **Black mulberry,** the infusion ingested of its leaves and the juice of the fruits acts in case of **intestinal inflammations** produced by bacteria, **parasites** or ingestion of some irritant product, **with belly pain,** even in the **presence of blood,** see **description of the plant.**

- **Bloodroot,** the infusion ingested controls **intestinal parasites and worms.** It acts **as a laxative** against constipation, see **description of the plant,** form of use **VII.**

- **Blue agave,** the infusion stimulates the growth of the **intestinal flora,** see **description of the plant.**

- **Boldo,** take infusions destroy the **ascaris or intestinal parasites** helping to deworm the body. **With great care** you can give children or young people obese a cup a day on an empty stomach. Warm with a crushed clove of raw garlic the effects are more potent, **caution,** see **description of plant.**

- **Breckland thyme,** the infusion ingested against **worms** and other **intestinal parasites,** see **description of the plant.**

- **Broadleaf cattail,** the infusion ingested its used to the **inflammation and ulceration of the large intestine,** see **description of the plant.**

- **Broadleaf plantain,** the infusion ingested or consumption **of their seeds** are **excellent** in making **intestinal parasites and worms disappear.** The **liquefaction** is used against **gastritis, intestines and irritable bowel,** see **description of the plant,** forms of use **VII and IX.**

- **Brussels sprout,** take 30 gr. of juice a day is very useful to eliminate **intestinal worms** of its germicidal power, see **description of the plant.**

- **Cacao,** it can act in a **dual way**, the **excess constipated**, but also serves as a relief to constipation, see **description of the plant.**

- **Calamus,** digestive **stimulant and laxative** used against constipation, see **description of the plant,** forms of use **VII and IX.**

- **Cantaloupe,** fruit of diuretic properties being a **mild laxative,** see **description of the plant.**

- **Carob tree,** can act as a laxative when regulating **intestinal transit** given its high content in **proteins, vegetables, fiber** and carbohydrates, vitamins A and group B, see **description of the plant.**

- **Chard,** its consumption maintains good **intestinal transit** and prevents **constipation,** see **description of the plant.**

- **Cherimoya,** low in fat and has fiber with the effect **of regulating the intestinal flora,** see **description of the plant.**

- **Chestnut fruit,** it is recommended **as a laxative** in those who suffer constipation, to consider their **dual property** by excess, see **description of the plant,** form of consume **VIII.**

- **Chickpea,** legume rich in fiber **for the intestine** and as **a laxative,** see **description of the plant,** form of use **VIII.**

- **Chilean myrtle,** the roots are used **for the intestine,** it's astringent, see **description of the plant,** form of use **VII.**

- **Cissampelos pareira,** it is effective for **parasites, worms,** infections and as an **intestinal stimulant.** It acts as a **laxative and purgative** in case of constipation, and **dual against dysentery,** see **description of the plant.**

- **Coconut,** its consumption because of the fiber content, it confers **properties certainly laxative,** see **description of the plant.**

- **Cowslip primrose,** the infusion ingested it is useful to treat **intestinal conditions** and against constipation as **a laxative,** see **description of the plant,** form of use **VII.**

- **Dyer's greenweed,** the infusion ingested of 15 gr. of flowers, serves **as a moderate laxative,** see **description of the plant.**

- **Eastern black walnut,** the infusion of the cortex has the ability to attack **parasitic and bacterial infections of the intestines** and to destroy **parasites such as worms,** see **description of the plant.**

- **Elms,** infusion for **irritable bowel** syndrome **and enteritis,** see **description of the plant,** form of use **VII.**

- **Erythraea chilensis,** good **stomach tonic.** Eliminates **intestinal worms,** see **description of the plant,** form of use **VII.**

- **Escarole,** its consumption its used as a **laxative,** see **description of plant.**

- **Fenugreek,** as **a laxative** for constipation, see **description of the plant,** forms of use and consume **VII and VIII.**

- **Fiddle dock,** it is consumed as depurative to eliminate **intestinal toxins,** and by its properties it acts **as a laxative,** see **description of the plant.**

- **Fig,** as **a laxative,** 50 gr. should be boiled for 20 minutes. of dried figs. On an empty stomach, drink the liquid and eat the boiled figs, see **description of the plant.**

- **Garlic,** helps to fight and eliminate **constipation,** deworm and eliminate **the annoying worms,** see **description of the plant.**

- **Grapefruit,** its consumption is good to speed up the **intestinal tract,** see **description of the plant.**

- **Grapevine,** the infusion of the ingested dry leaves for **intestinal hemorrhages** it is necessary to boil during ¼ of hour three **...Continue**

... spoonfuls of dried leaves crumbled per liter of water. Take 2 or 3 glasses every day, it helps stop the bleeding, see **description of the plant.**

- **Green pepper,** good for bowel function and diseases of the **gastrointestinal tract** due to its magnesium and fiber content, it prevents constipation as **a mild laxative,** see **description of the plant.**

- **Grenadia,** consumed **with seeds** has a high fiber content, very beneficial for health as **a laxative,** see **description of the plant.**

- **Hazel,** improves the functioning of the **intestinal transit** and **inflammation of the large intestine** (better after eating), see **description of the plant,** form of use **VII.**

- **Hazelnut,** the manganese and fiber can **promote digestion, intestinal transit** and elimination of toxins, see **description of the plant.**

- **Honey,** against the toxins that accumulate in your organism **(use from 1 year),** destroys microorganisms and helps improve **bowel function** and acts as **a laxative,** see **description of the Honey.**

- **Hops,** the infusion ingested (any form), is recommended to treat **irritable bowel syndrome, diverticulitis, Crohn's disease,** see **description of the plant,** forms of use **VII.**

- **Horehound,** the infusion ingested its used **against intestinal worms,** see **description of the plant.**

- **Ivy,** the infusion ingested it has a **laxative effect** avoiding constipation, see **description of the plant.**

- **Jamaica pepper,** contains "eugenol", which acts as an **intestinal analgesic,** relieving pain and **stomach upset,** see **description of the plant.**

- **Jasmine,** drinking jasmine tea improves **intestinal resistance,** see **description of the plant.**

- **Jujube,** the fruit contains abundant mucilages that form in **the intestine, being laxative**. For **intestinal irritation it is prepared with:** 60 gr. of fruit boil 20 minutes in a liter of water. Strain and sweeten to taste, preferably with honey. Take 5 to 6 tablespoons a day, see **description of the plant.**

- **Kaki fruit,** consumed **very mature,** is an excellent laxative for its fiber and sugars content, see **description of the plant.**

- **Kelp,** consumption due to its high content of vegetable fiber improves **transit and intestinal discomfort,** acting as **a laxative** in constipation problems, see **description of the plant.**

- **Kiwi,** its consumption for its content of magnesium and soluble and insoluble fiber, it confers strong properties, **improving intestinal transit,** and against constipation as **a good laxative**, see **description of the plant.**

- **Kudzu,** the consumption is **dual acting** acts as **a laxative** in case of constipation, but also as an antidiarrheal when **regenerating the intestinal flora,** see **description of the plant.**

- **Leek,** its consumption, by the fiber, acts **as a laxative** for constipation, see **description of the plant.**

- **Lemon,** its consumption against **intestinal parasites and worms,** also solves mild constipation as **a laxative,** see **description of the plant.**

- **Lentil,** its consumption is convenient against constipation **when being laxative,** and to **avoid irritable bowel síndrome,** see **description of plant.**

- **Loosestrife,** infusion **without sweetening or in enemas,** effectively helps to cure **dysentery, irritable bowel syndrome and hemorrhagic enteritis,** see **description of the plant.**

- **Mallow,** its consumption its used to constipation as **a laxative,** see **description of the plant.**

- **Mango,** as a food helps prevent constipation as **a laxative** and promote regularity and **intestinal health,** see **description of the plant.**

- **Marsh mallow,** the infusion ingested **of the leaves and roots** helps to reduce the inflammation associated with **and the intestine, enteritis, Crohn's disease, irritable bowel syndrome,** see **description of the plant.**

- **Mexican pepperleaf,** the infusion ingested combat **constipation,** see **description of the plant.**

- **Mint,** the infusion ingested it has strong antiseptic and antiparasitic properties, **for worms,** see **description of the plant.**

- **Muskmelon,** its consumption acts as a **mild laxative (consume with moderation under 6 years),** see **description of the plant.**

- **Naranjilla,** its consumption is good for the **pepsin** that is found exclusively in this fruit **being laxative** to eliminate constipation, soften the stool, relieves gas or flatulence and is quite beneficial in the gastrointestinal tract. It contains a large dose of vitamin D, which **helps strengthen the intestine** by facilitating its work of absorbing nutrients, such as calcium and proteins, see **description of the plant.**

- **Nettle,** it is used **in bowel problems and as a laxative,** it contains mucilage, fiber for bowel movement(peristaltics) to contract the muscles, causing the food bolus to pass faster to the excretory system. Drink an infusion with two tablespoons of dried leaves per liter of water before meals or three times a day, see **description of the plant.**

- **Oats,** due to its fibre content it is a **very good laxative,** being a softener of the gastric mucosa, **increasing intestinal transit,** and acts as a metabolic regulator, see **description of the plant,** form of use **VII.**

- **Olive oil,** its consumption helps as **a laxative** by its power for constipation. It is consume bread with oil regularly, at breakfast or snack, or a spoonful on an empty stomach, see **description of the Olive oil.**

- **Orange,** the infusion ingested of its leaves favors the elimination of toxic intestinal bacteria, and the **recovery of the "positive" intestinal flora. As a laxative** it is used **consumed or in juice with pulp** thanks to its fiber and magnesium content, see **description of the plant.**

- **Oregano,** the infusion **ingested** for **intestinal spasms,** see **description of the plant,** form of use **VII.**

- **Pansy,** the infusion ingested it has small **laxative** properties, being useful to treat cases of **constipation,** see **description of the plant.**

- **Papaya,** the consumption **from 3 years,** for its great contribution in fiber helps to **improve intestinal transit,** ideal fruit **as a laxative** and to **eliminate worms and pinworms,** see **description of the plant,** form of use **VII.**

- **Parsley,** good its consumption by the fiber content at the time of regularizing **the intestinal transit, and as a laxative** it is recommended to drink **a cup of parsley infusion**, before the 3 main meals, see **description of the plant.**

- **Passion fruit,** the consumption for its content in a high amount of fiber improves the **intestinal transit** being **laxative,** see **description of the plant.**

- **Pea,** insoluble fiber food beneficial **for lazy intestines,** being effective as a laxative, see **description of the plant.**

- **Pineapple,** very effective **as a laxative** on an empty stomach, **repeat** when constipation returns, see **description of the plant,** form of use **IX.**

- **Pollen,** it plays a regulatory role in **intestinal functions,** preventing and treating cases of constipation as **a laxative,** see **description of the Pollen,** forms of consume **VIII (2 and 3).**

- **Pomegranate,** its consumption its used to eliminate **intestinal parasites and worms,** see **description of the plant,** form of consume **VIII.**

- **Potato,** it is convenient for the significant amount of fiber, helping in **the regularity** of the stomach, **being laxative,** see **description of the plant.**

- **Prunus,** the infusion of the flowers, ingested, is a good tonic that improves and **purifies the intestine.** The plum compote **purifies the intestine,** as well as the fruit **(plum),** of **great laxative power** for people **with habitual constipation,** see **description of plant,** form of consume **VIII.**

- **Pumkin,** the **juice** of its pulp taken in the morning, on an empty stomach. **For the intestines,** peel pumpkin seeds, crush and mix with water or milk, it is an anthelmintic (to fight **intestinal parasites** such as ténia or solitary), see **description of the plant.**

- **Rooibos,** of **dual effect** should be **monitored in the smallest,** suitable in **case of diarrhea or constipation,** see **description of the plant.**

- **Roselle plant,** the infusion ingested improves the general functioning of the **intestines** with benefit **for digestions.** Effective as **a laxative in case of painful constipation,** see **description of the plant.**

- **Rye,** its contribution of fiber and mucilages favors the intestinal transit as **a laxative** by softening the mucous membranes. **Being dual** can act as an antidiarrheal, see **description of the plant,** form of consume **VIII.**

- **Saturn peaches,** its consumption by fiber content, **it is laxative,** regulates intestinal transit and prevents constipation, see **description of the plant.**

- **Soursop,** wonderful amebicide that fights **the parasites, and the intestinal worm,** see **description of the plant.**

- **Sowthistle,** the juice of the stem, drunk, is used as **a laxative** for constipation, see **description of the plant,** form of consume **VIII.**

- **Spearmint,** the infusion ingested, **from 6 years old,** it is **relaxing** in the muscles of **the intestine,** prevents **spasms and dyspepsia,** see **description of the plant.**

- **Spiked loosestrife,** the infusion ingested against **irritable bowel syndrome, enteritis,** see **description of the plant.**

- **Strawberry plant,** the infusion of its leaves and roots is used as **a laxative** for constipation, see **description of the plant,** form of use **VII.**

- **Sugarcane,** the juice is particularly useful in the treatment of the problem of **constipation,** see **description of the plant,** form of use **IX.**

- **Tamarind,** for its high fiber content it is very suitable and effective to **fight constipation.** Ideal for **lazy bowel** or colon problems, see **description of the plant,** form of use **VII.**

- **Tamarisk,** ingested decoction is used to combat **intestinal worms,** see **description of the plant.**

- **Tangerina,** its consumption it is excellent as **a laxative** to improve **intestinal transit,** also in juice, see **description of the plant.**

- **Tansy,** apply poultices of the leaves on the belly to **fight the worms.** In **the smallest or babies** to realize frictions with their oil on the belly, see **description of the plant.**

- **Thyme,** taken in tisane, and in the form of enema, helps to expel the pinworms **(tiny worms)** that children suffer. Prepare an infusion in ½ liter of water with 2 tablespoons of thyme. Boil 10 minutes. Strain and drink on an empty stomach without sweetening for a week, **avoiding bread and refined sugars.** The normal infusion ingested is antiseptic to help the **intestinal tract as a mild laxative,** see **description of the plant.**

- **Tomato,** of dual effect for **constipation and diarrhea (it is advisable to monitor their consumption in the smallest),** see **description of the plant.**

- **Turnip,** very digestive food for the **stomach,** helps improve **intestinal transit, considered a mild laxative,** see **description of the plant.**

- **Vanilla,** the infusion ingested is **a mild laxative,** see **description of plant.**

- **Verdolaga,** against **intestinal parasites and worms,** take 100 gr. of liquefied fresh plant in the mornings, for 4 or 5 days. It also serves the decoction of its seeds, see **description of the plant.**

- **Walnut tree,** its leaves in infusion fight **the parasites and worms of the intestine,** see **description of the plant,** form of use **VII.**

- **Watermelon,** you can use the seeds, they are edible and **of strong laxative action,** see **description of the plant.**

- **Wheat,** the consumption by its fiber acts **as a laxative** to relieve constipation, see **description of the plant.**

- **White pepper,** the consumption **(cooked in powder),** helps to **favor the intestinal transit** being a **mild laxative,** see **description of the plant.**

- **Yam,** for the treatment of intestinal diverticulosis disorders **(over 6 years old),** see **description of the plant.**

- **Yellow pepper,** because of its fiber content as **a laxative** facilitates the excretion of feces, see **description of the plant.**

- **Yellow trumpetbush,** the infusion ingested it is a vermifuge that helps **to expel intestinal worms,** see **description of the plant.**

- **Zucchini,** due to its high fiber content, it **is recommended** as a **laxative to limit its consumption in children** who have stomach problems with diarrhea. It acts against **intestinal** infections and parasites such **as worms, irritable colon, Crohn's disease,** see **description of the plant.**

Lice - Nits - Stings

Never replace the medication by the natural remedies. These remedies are supported, **you should always consult with your child's doctor.**
Continue on next page

- **Aloe vera,** relieves stinging and itching caused **by stings of insects, jellyfish or even nettles,** see **description of the plant.**

- **Apple,** in topical use by the poultice of an apple mush against **the stings of insects,** see **description of the plant.**

- **Bitter wood,** in topical use your vinegar is used effectively to treat and prevent **pediculosis (lice and nits),** and can be used every day as it contains no chemicals, see **description of the plant.**

- **Broadleaf plantain,** heat the leaves and in poultices are used for **insect stings,** see **description of the plant.**

- **Cissampelos pareira,** for **dog bites and rabies,** is used in tincture or crushed leaf with alcohol applied directly on the wound, see **description of the plant.**

- **Coconut,** see **tea tree**, see **description of the plant.**

- **Cornstarch,** for irritation or redness **from insect stings** and other skin problems. Prepare a thick mixture of cornstarch and water and apply to affected areas, see **description of the plant Corn and of the Cornstarch.**

- **Eucalyptus,** see **tea tree**, see **description of the plant.**

- **Oregano,** the **oil** is excellent against **insect stings,** applied directly on them, see **description of the plant.**

- **Pansy,** the infusion in washes or dressings has antimicrobial properties against **insect stings,** see **description of the plant.**

- **Patchouli,** a small amount in topical use, diluted in another oil, serves to **soothe insect stings,** see **description of the plant.**

- **Soursop,** the liquefaction **of the leaves** in topical use to eliminate **lice and nits,** applied to the scalp, see **description of the plant.**

- **Tansy,** against inflammations from **insect stings,** mix 30 drops of tincture diluted in 125 ml of water, to apply on the affected area, see **description of the plant.**

- **Tea tree,** against **lice or nits,** make a small mixture of oils with a tablespoon of coconut vegetable oil and add two drops of eucalyptus essential oil and two drops of tea tree essential oil. **Apply on the edges of the scalp,** following the hairline (ears, temples, forehead, and nape). But if you do not have all the oils, with the tea tree it will be enough, see **the different descriptions of the plants.**

- **Verdolaga,** the infusion by poultice or dressing acts as a soothing agent for stings, see **description of the plant.**

- **Walnut tree,** the infusion of its leaves in washes or dressings **for insect stings,** see **description of the plant,** form of use **VII.**

- **White clover,** in topical use, of plasters or compresses, is useful **for insect stings,** see **description of the plant.**

Memory and Cognitive action

Never replace the medication by the natural remedies. These remedies are supported, **you should always consult with your child's doctor.**

To avoid caries problems, when using ingested infusions, it is advisable, if necessary, to sweeten, use any sweetener that is indicated in the **Sweeteners** section.

- **Acorn,** as food to improve **memory,** see **description of the plant.**

- **Azuki red beans,** the contribution of group B vitamins and phosphorus makes strengthens memory and concentration, see **description of plant.**

- **Banana,** for **memory** has a very positive effect at the brain level, an investigation showed that students who eat banana in the morning have a **better concentration** throughout the day, see **description of the plant.**

- **Blackberry,** its consumption is very useful as a cognitive and neuroprotective enhancer **for memory,** see **description of the plant.**

- **Carob tree,** facilitates cognitive functions, **learning and memory improvement,** due to its high content of potassium, magnesium, phosphorus, zinc. **Excellent** during the growth stages, see **description of the plant.**

- **Carrot,** being rich in potassium and phosphorus, it is an excellent energizer **for tired minds,** see **description of the plant.**

- **Cherimoya,** it contains phosphorus that contributes to **reinforce the memory of students,** see **description of the plant.**

- **Cherry,** it is known as **"brain food",** it helps in your health and in the **prevention of memory loss,** see **description of the plant.**

- **Escarole,** its consumption is beneficial for the **mental function** by its concentration in folates, see **description of the plant.**

- **Evening primrose,** the oil is used **for memory** treating the syndrome that causes **lack of concentration,** see **description of the plant.**

- **Honey,** consumed daily **(from 1 year),** with water and empty stomach brings much vitality to the organism and **increases brain activity for memory,** see **description of the Honey.**

- **Indian pennywort,** it is effective in improving neuronal dendritic growth and against Gilles de la Tourette syndrome. **Very useful in lack of child care,** see **description of the plant.**

- **Lychee,** its consumption plays a role in brain health, **for memory,** necessary for certain neurotransmitters, see **description of the plant.**

- **Mango,** its consumption regular is good for the abundance of vitamin B6, essential for the proper **functioning of the brain,** and glutamine **especially improves memory and concentration,** see **description of plant.**

- **Nut,** the consumption of nuts is useful to maintain **good memory** and intelligence, see **description of the plant.**

- **Olive oil,** it has the ability to encourage the **development of the brain,** as well **as the olive.** There is a lower incidence of dementia in regions where people consume it on a regular basis, see **description of Olive oil.**

- **Oregano,** the infusion **ingested** promotes **blood circulation,** improving **brain irrigation** and **memory,** see **description of the plant,** form of use **VII.**

- **Pea,** food beneficial **for memory** by providing a large amount of magnesium, element that combats mental fatigue and helps in times of increased nervous stress by studies, see **description of the plant.**

- **Pollen,** improves **the mental** within the framework of normal or more intense activities, **generates greater intellectual efficiency (preparation of exams),** see **description of the Pollen,** forms of consume **VIII (2 and 3).**

- **Potato,** contains choline, a very important and versatile nutrient, **helping learning and memory,** see **description of the plant.**

- **Sunflower,** ideal for studying or taking an exam, because of its potassium and magnesium. Eating a handful of pipes, **improves concentration, memory and mental performance** in general, see **description of the plant.**

- **Tamarillo,** the **juice of this fruit,** twice a day is good for **the memory and the brain in general,** see **description of the plant.**

- **Thyme,** the infusion ingested it is a very vigorous tonic for both the physical, mental and emotional level **improving memory, see description of the plant.**

Mucosities - Phlegm

Never replace the medication by the natural remedies. These remedies are supported, **you should always consult with your child's doctor**.

To avoid caries problems, when using ingested infusions, it is advisable, if necessary, to sweeten, use any sweetener that is indicated in the **Sweeteners** section.

- **Asafoetida,** use the powder as a condiment or diluted in water or juice, is expectorant for **phlegm, see description of the plant.**

- **Bay laurel,** the infusion promotes the expulsion of **mucus and phlegm** in the respiratory tract in the case of **bronchitis, see description of plant.**

- **Chalk milkwort,** its used the infusion against the mucus, see **description of the plant.**

- **Coriander,** powerful expectorant eliminating **phlegm and mucus** consumed regularly, see **description of the plant.**

- **Elder,** the infusion used **in inhalations** is effective for coughing **with phlegm,** see **description of the plant.**

- **Elms,** the infusion ingested helps to **expel** secretions **and mucus** from the nose, see **description of the plant,** form of use **VII.**

- **Eucalyptus**, the inhalation is a powerful mucolytic with expectorant properties that fluidize the pulmonary secretions of **phlegm and mucus.** Another option to see in tea tree, see **description of the plant.**

- **Ginger,** against **the phlegm** cut the ginger into very thin slices and put in a jar of honey. Take a spoonful of that honey **(in older than 1 year),** in the morning and in and at nigth, see **description of plant and of Honey.**

- **Honeysuckle,** the infusion ingested it is an excellent complement when mixed with ginger (mucolytic and anti-inflammatory) for **mucus,** to be complemented, see **description of the plant.**

- **Horehound,** the infusion ingested it helps to expel **mucus and phlegm,** see **description of the plant.**

- **Lemon verbena,** the infusion ingested or in inhalations it is useful for the respiratory system in **expelling mucus,** see **description of the plant.**

- **Lungwort,** the infusion ingested its used to facilitate the expectoration of **phlegm and bronchial mucus,** by the saponin it contains, see **description of the plant,** form of use **VII.**

- **Malabar nut,** the infusion ingested of the whole plant is used **in older than 3 years,** as an expectorant **for phlegm,** see **description of the plant.**

- **Mallow,** the infusion ingested being rich **in mucilage,** it is ideal to **soften mucus,** see **description of the plant.**

- **Mint,** the infusion ingested removes secretions such as **phlegm and mucus** from the respiratory tract, see **description of the plant.**

- **Myrtle,** the infusion ingested **(in older than 6 years),** and in inhalations to clean bronchial secretions such as **phlegm and mucus,** also in inhalations, see **description of the plant,** form of use **VII.**

- **Pansy,** the infusion ingested to eliminate **phlegm,** and soften **mucous membranes** by their expectorant principles, see **description of the plant.**

- **Radish,** in **older than 3 years, removes excess mucus** in the organism, see **description of the plant.**

- **Rye,** used as daytime water is useful due to its mucilages, to soothe and soften the **mucous membranes and phlegm** of the respiratory system, see **description of the plant,** form of use **VII.**

- **Safflower,** the infusion ingested in Hindu medicine, its flowers are used for chest pains by congestion, relieving and softening phlegm and mucus, see **description of the plant.**

- **Sage,** the inhalation of a decoction of sage leaves can be used for coughing **with phlegm,** see **description of the plant.**

- **Sanicle,** the infusion ingested for cases of **excess mucus or thick mucus,** see **description of the plant.**

- **Spearmint,** the infusion ingested, **from 6 years,** is beneficial in the elimination of **mucus,** see **description of the plant.**

- **Tamarillo,** good to control **mucus,** taking at least twice a day the juice of this fruit, see **description of the plant.**

- **Tea of Aragon,** the infusion fights the mucus, see **description of plant.**

- **Tea tree,** for **phlegm, mucus,** inhalation of eucalyptus, **elder flower** and 2 or 3 drops of **tea tree essence,** is very effective, see **descriptions plants.**

- **Thyme,** the infusion helps **eliminate mucus,** see **description of plant.**

- **Tree lungwort,** the infusion it has a balsamic effect and is a **good mucolytic,** see **description of the plant,** form of use **VII.**

- **Virginia water horehound,** the infusion ingested it helps to expel **mucus and phlegm,** in places where bacteria and other pathogens can develop, see **description of the plant.**

- **West Indian cherry,** consuming the fruit helps to reduce **mucus,** see **description of the plant.**

Oral diseases - Teeth /Gums

Never replace the medication by the natural remedies. These remedies are supported, **you should always consult with your child's doctor**.

To avoid caries problems, when using ingested infusions, it is advisable, if necessary, to sweeten, use any sweetener that is indicated in the **Sweeteners** section.

- **Agrimony,** la infusión in **mouthwash** helps the healing of **inflammations in the mouth.** It is made by boiling 100 gr. of dried leaves and flowers in a liter of water, rest and use **without sweetening,** see **description of plant.**

- **Aloe vera,** chewing a piece of branch/leaf can remove some stains on **the teeth and whiten them,** favor the good **health of the gums**. Combat **tartar** by chewing a piece for a few minutes, several times a week. Chew or put a piece on **the tooth** to avoid pain, see **description of the plant.**

- **Annato tree,** in **mouth inflammations** take an infusion with a bunch of annatto and a tablespoon of ginger dessert, boiled in a liter of water, rinse every 8 hours at least, see **the different descriptions of the plants.**

- **Apple,** for the **cracks in the lips,** prepare 100 gr. of grated apples and 100 gr. of butter, apply over the cracks during the night, see **description of the plant.**

- **Asafoetida,** a piece mixed with lemon juice does **wonders for toothache,** see **description of the plant.**

- **Bergamot orange,** the diluted oil or the infusion, with antimicrobial substances, is used in **mouthwashes** against any **oral infection,** see **description of the plant.**

- **Bistort,** the infusion its used to **mouth inflammations** in mouthwash, see **description of the plant,** forms of use **VII and IX.**

- **Blackberry plant,** the infusion of its leaves in topical use fights **ulcers or sores** in the mouth, **canker sores, gum problems** (in rinses, **without sweetening**). **Ingested** acts **against tongue inflammations** (also in rinses, without sweetening), see **description of the plant.**

- **Bloodroot,** the infusion acts **against cavities in rinses**, see **description of the plant,** form of use **VII.**

- **Broadleaf plantain,** the infusion in **mouthwashes for oral conditions heals wounds of the mouth and gums,** see **description of the plant,** form of use **VII.**

- **Calamus,** chewing its fresh roots fights and **reaffirms bleeding gums,** bad breath or halitosis, see **description of the plant.**

- **Carrot,** the fluorine present is fundamental for the state of **the tooth enamel** and to avoid the **appearance of cavities.** Raw **strengthens teeth and gums, improves oral blood** supply and prevents bacteria from sticking to teeth, see **description of the plant.**

- **Catnip,** chewing the plant **relieves the toothache,** see **description plant.**

- **Clementina,** strengthens **the gums** in case of gingivitis, see **description of the plant.**

- **Chestnut tree,** to strengthen **the teeth,** see **description of the plant,** forms of use **VII (1 and 3).**

- **Chilean myrtle,** it is used in gargles and rinses, **without sweetening,** to improve **sores, mouth wounds, gums,** see **description of the plant,** form of use **VII.**

- **Durmast oak,** the infusion ingested in gargles as an antiseptic, it is used **for gums,** and in mouthwash to **combat gingivitis,** see **description of the plant,** form of use **VII.**

- **Eastern black walnut,** the chewed crust, with its powerful astringent properties, **relieves toothaches.** The infusion of the crust **in topical use** its used to the **treatment of cold sores,** see **description of the plant.**

- **Fig tree,** the infusion by swishing with half a fig leaf is used against inflammations of **the gums, gingivitis and pyorrhea** (warm swishing in case of inflamed gums or prepare a tea by adding lemon, cinnamon, or mixing with another type of tea). Also for **neuralgia and toothache,** see **the different descriptions of the plants.**

- **Garden nasturtium,** the infusión or decoction in mouthwash, for **canker sores, ulcers and inflammations,** see **description of the plant,** form of use **VII.**

- **Geranium or Cranesbills,** the infusion in mouthwashes for oral affections, see **description of the plant,** form of use **VII.**

- **Ginger,** against **toothache,** cut a piece of root and chew in the area of pain, you will notice a great relief, see **description of the plant.**

- **Gladiolus,** its **fresh rhizome** is used **to reduce inflammation and relieve gum pain in children during teething,** see **description of the plant.**

- **Herb Bennet,** in mouthwash to **tighten bloody gums** and to hold **teeth and the toothache,** see **description of the plant,** form of use **VII (2).**

- **Horse-chestnut,** the infusion of its leaves improves **gingivitis and teeth** processes (in mouthwash **without sweetening**). In tablets **the dosage would be equivalent to two capsules a day (see leaflet),** see **description of the plant.**

- **Horsetail,** in mouthwash fights **gum bleeding and gingivitis,** see **description of the plant,** form of use **VII.**

- **Indian pennywort,** the infusion ingested and mouthwashes **(for over 6 years),** it is effective for the treatment of chronic periodontitis, **without sweetening,** in **teeth and gums,** see **description of the plant.**

- **Kinnikinnick,** the infusion of its leaves for mouthwash and gargles, **without sweetening,** its used to **fight mouth inflammations,** see description of the plant.

- **Large-leaved lime,** the infusion ingested and in rinses **(without sweetening)** prevents the appearance **of annoying cavities** and as an antiseptic reduces **inflammation of the gums,** see **description of the plant.**

- **Linden tree,** boil a cup of water with a handful of its flowers, or about 6 leaves in its absence. Rest 5 minutes, strain and **use for rinsing** or gargle before bedtime, **without sweetening,** see **description of the plant.**

- **Lychee,** its consumption its used to **relieve dry mouth and keep gums healthy,** see **description of the plant.**

- **Marsh mallow,** the **root extracts** are used as a mouthwash to treat inflammations, and in **the first dentition** to reduce irritation, see description of the plant.

- **Martagon lily,** the infusion ingested or in topical use (rinses), as well as the tincture have sedative and analgesic effects, for the pain of different origin **in teeth and molars,** see **description of the plant.**

- **Myrtle,** in rinses **(in older than 6 years),** it is used in **oral affections** for recurrent aphthous stomatitis (RAS), painful disorder. Also for the **ulcerative of the oral cavity** for unknown cause, see **description of the plant,** form of use **VII.**

- **Oregano,** the infusion in **rinses and locutions** for oral problems, gums, and type of odontalgias, teeth pain and toothaches, see **description of the plant,** form of use **VII.**

- **Passion fruit,** its consumption intervenes in the formation of collagen, beneficial **for tooth strengthening, see description of the plant.**

- **Perforate St John's-wort,** the infusion ingested or in gargles is used **for oral, dental infections. Encapsulated powder** can also be used, see **description of the plant,** form of use **VII (1).**

- **Pomegranate,** the infusion mouthwashes with dry (inner) skin can help prevent problems such **as cavities.** Reduces **tartar from dental plaque** with antibacterial effects. In India the white and bitter parts of the pomegranate are used as ingredients in natural toothpastes. In **the gums it** helps to prevent problems such as periodontitis or gingivitis, see **description plant.**

- **Saffron,** a concentrate saffron with water in topical use and applied **to the molars** causes relief; it is also good for teething problems in children. Its components help prevent or cure **sores in the mouth,** making mouthwashes or "swish", see **description of the plant.**

- **Sanicle,** the infusion ingested in gargles or rinses it fights the **pharyngeal inflammations, gingivitis or bleeding gums, dental abscesses, and annoying canker sores on the lips,** see **description of the plant.**

- **Thyme,** the infusion in topical use for **mouth conditions** helps to treat and fight infections and inflammations such **as canker sores,** and others, washing the affected area during the day, and applying a wet cotton over the afta. **The infusion resulting** from boiling 50 gr. of thyme in 1 liter of water for 10 minutes its used to the care of **the teeth and against gum gingivitis,** make **warm rinses. The normal infusion** is very effective **to fight the halitosis,** see **description of the plant.**

- **Vanilla,** the infusion in rinses **(without sweetening)** to fight **oral and dental infections,** halitosis or **bad breath,** see **description of the plant.**

- **Verdolaga,** for **sensitive teeth and gums** it is good to chew the fresh plant, see **description of the plant.**

- **Walnut tree,** the infusion of its leaves, fights and prevents **mouth sores,** see **description of the plant,** form of use **VII.**

- **White nettle,** the infusion of the root in mouthwashes, **without sweetening,** is used for the **gums in case of gingivitis,** see **description of the plant.**

- **Yellow trumpetbush,** its used the infusion to treat **toothaches,** see description of the plant.

- **Finally,** we describe the plants that only **the simple infusion is necessary to ingest** or as in this case for rinses or gargles, without sweetening, in infections, bleeding gums, gingivitis, canker sores, pyorrhea, inflammations, **always one before sleeping** with:

Ajuga iva, Breckland thyme, Chamomile, Dyer's greenweed, Elder, Heath speedwell, Loosestrife, Marjoram, Mountain everlasting, Myrrh, Pansy, Spiked loosestrife.

If the infusion is going to be **used frequently,** its recommend **boiling the plant in a liter of water, or in the amount of water that we create** according to the daily use to be taken, thus way we will avoid time in its preparation and instead of the prepared bags that they sell you can buy in bulk to economize. It can **also be potentiated** with different plants for the same ailment, but it is convenient **to always remember** the perfect use of each plant used according **to its description,** in case there is any **interaction with drugs or possible contraindications.**

Refreshing - Water by day - Stomach - Vomiting

Never replace the medication by the natural remedies. These remedies are supported, **you should always consult with your child's doctor.**

Continue

To avoid caries problems, when using ingested infusions, it is advisable, if necessary, to sweeten, use any sweetener that is indicated in the **Sweeteners** section.

- **Barley,** for **stomach,** gastric and **intestinal alterations,** due to its enzymatic content in chlorophyll, vitamins and minerals. Excellent source of fiber that activates the **stomach digestive** system and keeps it healthy, **it aids in digestion,** assimilation and correct use by the digestive cells. Also used **as day water** the liquid can be added to the juices, or boiled with a cinnamon as a refreshing, see **description of the plant,** form of use **VII.**

- **Bay laurel,** the infusion ingested relieves **stomach discomfort**, reducing **intestinal spasms,** see **description of the plant.**

- **Beans,** the consumption of dried beans for **better digestion** is when sage or savory species are added to their preparation, see **the different descriptions of the plants.**

- **Bistort,** the infusion ingested is demulcent favors the functioning of the **stomach in case of stomatitis,** see **description of plant,** form of use **VII.**

- **Black mustard,** its consumption its a good **stomach digestive and in digestion**, sprinkled in the meals with assiduity. Its consumption **as intestinal purgative**: 15 gr. of black mustard crushed and dissolved in a glass of water, **to vomit,** see **description of the plant.**

- **Blackberry plant,** the juice of the fruits **is a refreshing and invigorating drink,** see **description of the plant.**

- **Carrot,** to fight **stomach pain from intoxication,** calming gastric discomfort, see **description of the plant.**

- **Chamomile,** the infusion ingested fights **stomach pain, flatus, gastritis, diverticulosis, diverticulitis.** In case of **ingestion of toxic** causes vomiting, see **description of the plant.**

- **Cinnamon with honey,** for **over 1 year,** the standard dose will be one dessert spoonful, mix with a little hot water, and it will taste like a sweetened infusion, or with cold water, and in this way it will be a **refreshing and healthy drink.** It can also be combined with juice, milk, yogurt, but always without cooking, see **description of plant and of Honey.**

- **Cissampelos pareira,** the infusion ingested acts in **bad digestions,** relieves **stomach pains, abdominals, stomach infections** and as a digestive stimulant, see **description of the plant.**

- **Clary sage,** to treat **digestion disorders,** relaxing the muscles of the digestive tract, **colic, stomach pains,** see **description of the plant.**

- **Dyer's greenweed,** the infusion ingested 15 gr. of flowers, **as a purgative,** is emetic for vomiting, its more pleasant to eat because it contains sugar, mucilages and a certain amount of vitamin C. Increase the dose in case of **stomach intoxications,** see **description of the plant.**

- **Herb Bennet,** its used to intestinal disorders, **gastroenteritis,** see **description of the plant,** form of use **VII (4).**

- **Iceland moss,** the double decoction ingested by cetrarico acid is especially useful in **processes with vomiting. The infusion** ingested in **any way indicated,** three cups a day is effective in **stomach gastroenteritis,** see **description of the plant,** form of use **VII.**

- **Jasmine,** drinking tea helps in the prevention of **stomach diseases,** see **description of the plant.**

- **Kiwi,** its consumption regular improves the functioning of the entire **tract digestive and stomach,** see **description of the plant.**

- **Kudzu,** consume help in gastrointestinal and **stomach problems** is recommended to **ingest in powder and not in tablets. ...Continue**

... Dissolve in a glass of water two tablespoons of dessert, boil 5 minutes until it acquires a gelatinous consistency of pinkish color. It has no flavor, you can drink it directly or add it to a fruit juice, see **description of plant.**

- **Lettuce,** drink your juice in **stomach problems,** see **description of plant.**

- **Linden tree,** ingested combats digestive and **stomach disorders,** see **description of the plant,** form of use **VII.**

- **Mallow,** the infusion ingested in the digestive system, is very effective **for the irritated stomach,** see **description of the plant.**

- **Mint,** the infusion ingested or its **essential oil** applied in front and temples, can reduce symptoms such as **nausea, vomiting.** The infusion ingested **in the stomach** causes a relaxing and anaesthetic action, acts especially in the **gastrointestinal tract** by favouring the digestive process **for colon irritation,** see **description of the plant.**

- **Naranjilla,** its consumption it is very good **for stomach digestive health,** as it contains a high amount of dietary fiber, that helps to push food through the digestive tract and also **relieves swelling,** see **description of the plant.**

- **Nettle,** its used in **stomach problems** to figth **poisoning** by ingestion of **molluscs or crustaceans.** Drink an infusion made with two tablespoons of dried leaves per liter of water, before meals or three times a day, see **description of the plant.**

- **Onion,** excellent source of fiber that **activates the digestive system** and keeps it healthy. The prebiotics present favor the development of beneficial bacteria that **help digestion.** Also drinking the resulting liquid by boiling it with a little honey **(only older than 1 year)** is used for **internal wounds,** see **description of the plant and of the Honey.**

- **Passion fruit,** the consumption reduces the risk of certain alterations and **digestive or stomach diseases,** see **description of the plant.**

- **Peach,** its juice, **moderately in children under 6 years,** helps digestive and stomach problems, see **description of the plant.**

- **Psoralea,** its consumption its used to **digestive discomforts and stomach pains,** see **description of the plant,** form of use **VII.**

- **Quince,** its consumption its used to the **stomach in gastrointestinal** infections, see **description of the plant.**

- **Rooibos,** the infusion ingested se utiliza for its usefulness in **alleviating the problems of nausea and vomiting,** see **description of the plant.**

- **Roselle plant,** the infusion it acts in the **stomach** against the **antispasmodic effects**, and against digestive discomforts **irritable bowel syndrome,** see **description of the plant.**

- **Sage,** the infusion ingested can be used **from 6 years, but never more than three daily infusions,** for **stomach relief in gastroenteritis with vomiting.** It also serves as a digestive support with the **beans,** see **the different descriptions of the plants.**

- **Salep drink,** recommended its consumption for the **stomach** in cases of **gastroenteritis,** as an **intestinal emollient,** against **dyspepsia** and all types of **inflammations** at this level, see **description of the plant.**

- **Sugarcane,** acts as a digestive, by the presence of potassium keeping it in good shape, prevents **stomach infections.** Also take 4 cups per day of decoction, it is an effective depurative, see **description of the plant,** form of use **IX.**

- **Summer savory,** serves as a digestive support with **the beans,** see **the different descriptions of the plants.**

- **Tamarind,** the infusion ingested is very effective to fight **digestive problems** and the **irritation of digestive mucous membranes,** as it is **purgative.** Cases of **indigestión or dysentery,** to figth **cases of vomiting,** see **description of the plant,** form of use **VII.**

- **Vanilla,** the infusion ingested relieves **stomach pain, gastritis** and other discomforts, see **description of the plant.**

- **Watermelon,** it should be consumed especially and more frequently in summer, due to the abundance in water being **refreshing and detoxifying** the body, see **description of the plant.**

- **Wheat,** its consumption for the **stomach** by B vitamins **help to metabolize** the food that is consumed and convert it into energy, see **description of the plant.**

- **Yellow trumpetbush,** the infusion ingested for **stomach pains,** gastritis, **indigestions,** see **description of the plant.**

- **Finally,** we describe the plants that only **the simple infusion is necessary to or the consumption**, in this case to favor digestive and stomach problems to deal with:
Agar Agar, Agrimony, Baccharises, Blue agave, Cacao, Catnip, Cherry, Chicory, Clementina, Hazelnut, Lamb´s lettuce, Lemon verbena, Narrow-leaf strap fern, Peanut, Saffron, Sowthistle, Summer savory. If the infusion is going to be **used frequently,** its recommend **boiling the plant in a liter of water, or in the amount of water that we create** according to the daily use to be taken, thus way we will avoid time in its preparation and instead of the prepared bags that they sell you can buy in bulk to economize. It can **also be potentiated** with different plants for the same ailment, but it is convenient **to always remember** the perfect use of each plant used according **to its description,** in case there is any **interaction with drugs or possible contraindications.**

Respiratory problems
Bronchitis - Congestions - Colds - Coughs

Never replace the medication by the natural remedies. These remedies are supported, **you should always consult with your child's doctor**.

To avoid caries problems, when using ingested infusions, it is advisable, if necessary, to sweeten, use any sweetener that is indicated in the **Sweeteners** section

- **Almond,** For lung **pulmonary congestion and bronchitis,** take 30 grated almonds with sweetened water. For **whooping cough** mix two tablespoons of honey, with two of almond oil, **take for 1 week morning and night,** see **description of the plant and of the Honey.**

- **Anacahuita,** highly recommended to cure **respiratory conditions and bronchial inflammations.** It is expectorant **to relieve cough,** take very hot 4 or 5 times a day, see **description of the plant,** form of use **VII.**

- **Annato tree,** to **relieve and cure bronchitis and cough,** take 1 gr. its dust powder in a cup of hot water, see **description of the plant.**

- **Asafoetida,** used since antiquity for infections and as a respiratory stimulant **relieving chest congestion.** It has the power to alleviate **problems of asthma, bronchitis, dry cough, whooping cough,** mixed with a little honey (**in older than 1 year**) and ginger, see **description of the different plants and of the Honey.**

- **Ash,** the infusion ingested its used for **colds,** see **description of plant.**

- **Banana,** studies indicate that children who eat at least one banana a day reduce the probality of developing **asthma** by 34%, see **description plant.**

- **Bay laurel,** the infusion ingested acts on the respiratory tract, mainly in case of **bronchitis, see description of the plant.**

- **Bergamot orange,** its used against **cough** (gargles). For **bronchitis,** applying the balm of your oil through inhalation, gargle and massage will get a prompt recovery, see **description of the plant.**

- **Bigheaded / Conehead thyme,** the infusion ingested its used to fight **bronchial inflammations** and against **whooping cough.** The infusion **with honey (from 1 year),** against **colds,** see **description of the plant.**

- **Bistort,** the infusion ingested for treatment **of colds,** see **description of the plant,** form of use **VII.**

- **Bitter lettuce,** very used syrup against: **bronchitis,** calm and suppress cough (whooping cough), see **description of the plant.**

- **Black mustard,** its consumption as an **antiinflammatory** it is effective in the treatment of internal organs and in respiratory diseases such as **bronchitis, pulmonary congestion, colds,** see **description of the plant.**

- **Black pepper,** the infusion ingested, without excess, relieves **respiratory processes, congestion,** symptoms of **colds and cough** (in this case of black pepper half a lemon and suck), see **description of the different plants.**

- **Blackberry plant,** the **consumption or the juice of the blackberry** due to its high content of vitamins A and C, it is essential to prevent **infections of the respiratory tract** and catarrhs **such as colds,** see **description plant.**

- **Blackberry,** for **respiratory problems,** its fruits must be used. **In case of cough,** drink a cup of hot water in which a teaspoon of the artisanal syrup will have been added. **Against the cold the dried blackberries** are a great source of proteins, vitamin C and K, fiber and iron. **As a food,** it is suitable to avoid catarrh and support against certain viral diseases, see **description of the plant,** form of consume **VIII.**

- **Breckland thyme,** the infusion ingested its used against the **cough and whooping cough,** see **description of the plant.**

- **Broadleaf plantain,** the infusion acts against **chronic bronchitis.** Quite effective in **processes of flu.** It is antitussive and **expectorant in colds and coughs,** see **description of the plant,** form of use **VII.**

- **Brussels sprout,** its vitamin C for the respiratory system helps to reduce the **symptoms of the cold,** see **description of the plant.**

- **Catnip,** the infusion its used to treatment of respiratory problems of **colds and coughs,** see **description of the plant.**

- **Cecropia,** the infusion it is considered an **antiasthmatic** and solves problems in the airways such as **bronchitis or pneumonia, pneumonia, pulmonary emphysema,** to **relieve cough and colds** (associated with the lungwort plant), see **the different descriptions of the different plants,** form of use **VII.**

- **Chachacoma,** to fight **convulsive cough, the syrup** is excellent, you should **consult the doctor or specialist how to use it.** Generally, patients begin to feel relief from the third day of treatment. **With lungwort** and ingested, it is used **to fight and relieve colds,** see **description of different plants,** form of use **VII.**

- **Chalk milkwort,** the infusion ingested its used against **bronchial problems, congestion, lungs,** to fight **the flu, mucus, colds, cough,** see **description of the plant.**

- **Cherimoya,** in case of chronic diseases and to **fight colds,** see **description of the plant.**

- **Chestnut tree,** to fight **cough, whooping cough,** see **description of the plant,** form of use **VII (1).**

- **Chilean myrtle,** against the cold, take 3 times a day the infusion of two tablespoons full of dried leaves and ground by 1 liter of water, see **description of the plant.**

- **Cinnamon,** the infusion is high in vitamin C to **fight the cold,** see description of the plant.

- **Cinnamon with honey,** fights and **relieve colds (from one year),** see description of the plant and of the Honey.

- **Cissampelos pareira,** the infusion ingested it is useful in **case of colds.** It is of great **expectorant power in cough problems,** see **description plant.**

- **Clary sage,** the oil helps to **calm the spasms** and tightness of the muscles surrounding the **bronchi in asthmatics.** The ingested infusion relieves **the cold,** see **description of the plant,** forms of use **VII (7 and 8).**

- **Clementina,** rich in Vitamin C, B, citric acid and carotene, it stands out for its well-known **anti-cold effect,** see **description of the plant.**

- **Common milkwort,** the infusion ingested its used as an expectorant **against cough,** see **description of the plant.**

- **Coriander,** powerful expectorant **against cough,** eliminating phlegm and mucus consumed regularly during this process, see **description plant.**

- **Cowslip primrose,** the infusion ingested, even in gargling for airway problems, **colds or coughs,** see **description of the plant,** form of use **VII.**

- **Echinacea,** to fight diseases of the respiratory system such as **lung congestions, cold, cough,** even as a preventive you can take a daily infusion without any fear, **there are prepared for over 6 years,** see **description of the plant.**

- **Elder,** the infusion ingested it is beneficial **for colds** and as an **expectorant for cough, also in inhalations,** see **description of the plant.**

- **Elms,** the infusion is effective for **lung diseases** and to **fight cough,** see description of the plant, see form of use **VII.**

- **English primrose,** the infusion ingested its used against **tuberculosis,** see **description of the plant.**

- **Erythraea chilensis,** macerated is **effective in the first period of pneumonia, pleurisy,** see **description of the plant,** form of use **VII.**

- **Eucalyptus**, inhalations reduce inflammation, such as **anti-inflammatory,** facilitate breathing and improve the airways in **chest congestion the tracheitis,** as well as constipation **or colds.** Good inhibitor of bronchial irritation, **is recommended** in diseases such as **bronchitis, both acute and chronic.** Relieves **cough to be antitussive,** performed twice a day. **Its oil** is used for **nasal congestion,** as well as for **sinusitis (older than 6 years)** in support of the remedy with **Niaouli,** see **description of the different plants.**

- **European searocket,** the juice is used for being a good remedy against **bronchial catarrhs, pulmonary and colds,** see **description of the plant.**

- **Fenugreek,** it is beneficial against **congestion** and, above all, to counteract **colds and pharyngitis,** see **description of the plant,** forms of use **VII and VIII.**

- **Fig,** to fight **bronchitis and cough,** this plant to be emollient should be 15 to 20 dried figs reduced to pieces in 250 gr. milk, for about 20 minutes, add a teaspoonful of honey **(over 1 year old),** strain and drink the hot milk one cup a day before bedtime, use until the cough or cold disappears completely, see **description of plant and the Honey.**

- **Garden angelica,** the infusions of the leaves acts as a great natural expectorant, stimulating **the bronchial secretion and cough,** see **description of the plant.**

- **Garden nasturtium,** the infusion or decoction treats respiratory conditions and diseases such **as cough,** see **description of the plant,** form of use **VII.**

- **Garden yellow loosestrife,** the infusion **against cough** drink a cup sweetened with honey **(over 1 year),** take 2 or 3 times a day, see **description of the plant.**

- **Garlic,** it is advised in the coldest times of the year, when it is common for them to get **flu or colds,** see **description of the plant.**

- **Ginger,** the infusion with a little honey and asafetida, has the power to alleviate **bronchitis problems** and drinking **(the older than 1 year)** it serves in **bronchial problems.** It is also good expectorant **against cough, dry cough, whooping cough,** cut the ginger into very thin slices and put in a jar of honey **(in older than 1 year)** taking a spoonful of that honey in the morning and at night served **against coughing. For the cold** you can add cinnamon to the infusion of ginger with white flower honeysuckle, see **description of the different plants and of the Honey.**

- **Gladiolus,** the infusion its used **to relieve cough** and drink only one cup at night **in case of bronchitis,** see **description of the plant.**

- **Gum arabic tree,** the infusion helps to treat cases of **bronchitis** by forming a protective, soothing layer over **congested respiratory tract infections.** As a treatment **for cough.** For the **common cold,** in mild infections (also in gargles), see **description of the plant.**

- **Heath speedwell,** the infusion relieves **bronchitis** and fights **bronchiectasis,** as well as **catarrhs, colds and coughs,** see **description of the plant.**

- **Helychrysum,** against **bronchitis, pulmonary emphysema, and coug** (being expectorant), see **description of the plant.**

- **Honey,** taking honey only **the older than 1 years** is used against **bronchitis,** destroying microorganisms and **preventing cold.** It also supports the remedies of **Almond, Asafoetida, Bigheaded/Conehead thyme, Fig tree/Fig, Ginger, Jujube, Loosestrife,** see **description of the different plants and of Honey,** in case there are **interactions with medications or possible contraindications.**

- **Honeysuckle,** the infusion its used to **respiratory tract infections,** see **description of the plant,** form of use **VII.**

- **Horehound,** the infusion ingested for **the pains** and congestions **of the lungs, the cold** and respiratory affections, see **description of the plant.**

- **Iceland moss,** the infusion ingested in **any of the ways indicated,** taking three cups a day, it is especially indicated **in catarrhs processes or colds,** sweeten to taste. The confers **antitussive** action, see **description of the plant,** form of use **VII.**

- **Indian fig opuntia,** its consumption it is good for the **congestions and pains of lung diseases,** see **description of the plant.**

- **Ivy,** the infusion ingested **of its leaves** is used **in colds** of upper respiratory tract and **in treatment of chronic bronchitis, colds** and even in cases of **rebellious cough with vomiting** and as an expectorant for **irritative cough**. The infusion ingested **of its fruits** is used in **pulmonary hemoptysis** (blood expectoration), see **description of the plant.**

- **Jamaica pepper,** its consumption is used for chest **congestions** and relieve **bronchitis,** see **description of the plant.**

- **Jasmine,** tea **ingested and gargle** can prevent colds, and helps to have an earlier recovery, see **description of the plant.**

- **Jujube,** since ancient times it is considered **excellent anticatarral** and very beneficial for **chest congestion,** considered expectorant against **persistent cough,** it is used in **colds, acute bronchitis.** It is prepared with 60 gr. of the fruit, boiled for 20 minutes in a liter of water. Strain and sweeten to taste, preferably with honey (**from 1 year**), see **description of the plant.**

- **Kaki fruit,** effective **in preventing colds** due to their contribution in vitamins A and C in joint action, see **description of the plant.**

- **Kudzu,** its consumption relieves **bronchial processes,** helps to **reduce fever** and to relieve problems in the processes related to **colds and coughs,** see **description of the plant.**

- **Large-leaved lime,** the infusion ingested its used to reduce **attacks of cough** after a cold, see **description of the plant.**

- **Lavender,** its oil is used in **nasal congestion,** as well as for **sinusitis (older than 6 years),** in support of the remedy **with Niaouli,** see **description of the different plants.**

- **Leek,** its consumption acts in the **respiratory affections** and helps in **bronchial problems and intense cough,** see **description of the plant.**

- **Lemon,** its consumption **it is convenient** to provide vitamin C, **for colds,** see **description of the plant.**

- **Lemon grass,** the infusion ingested use the **elaborated sachets,** has antispasmodic expectorant properties for **cough,** and anticatarral **in colds,** see **description of the plant.**

- **Lemon verbena,** in inhalations against the affections of the respiratory system, expels mucus, and to **relieve cough,** see **description of the plant.**

- **Lettuce,** Drunk juice can help reduce **asthma symptoms,** and problems in the respiratory system, such as **bronchitis,** see **description of the plant.**

- **Lilac,** the infusion of the bark or flowers serves to alleviate **bronchitis,** and in **catarrh and colds,** see **description of the plant.**

- **Linden tree,** for its properties on the sweat glands (flavonoglucosides), as carminative and diaphoretic is used to be effective against **colds, and in catarrhal processes,** see **description of the plant,** form of use **VII.**

- **Lungwort,** the infusion ingested its used to soothe and treat **cough, and whooping cough.** Against the **bronchitis, colds,** the same infusion associated with Cecropia or Senecio oreophyton, it is successfully used in **inflammations of the bronchi and colds** in general, see **description of the different plants,** form of use **VII.**

- **Malabar nut,** the infusion ingested of the entire plant is used **in older than 3 years,** for **chronic infections** of the respiratory tract **such as bronchitis, cold and cough,** see **description of the plant.**

- **Mallow,** the infusion **ingested** its used in diseases of the **respiratory tract, for pain and congestion** in the chest. It is very effective **against bronchitis, in catarrhal processes, colds and dry cough,** see **description of the plant.**

- **Mango,** consuming **the peel can cure coughs and colds** as it is rich in phyto nutrients, antioxidants, carotenoids and polyphenols, see **description of the plant.**

- **Marsh mallow,** the infusion ingested of the **leaves and roots** are anti-inflammatory, **reduces the pain** and swelling associated with the mucous membranes of the airways, as in **bronchitis, the cases of cough,** see **description of the plant.**

- **Mexican pepperleaf,** the infusion ingested it is useful **against coughing, asthma, bronchitis and dyspnea** (difficulty breathing), see **description plant.**

- **Mint,** the infusion ingested it is refreshing, **decongestant of** the respiratory tract, **fights colds, coughs** and typical ailments caused by the cold, see **description of the plant.**

- **Mountain everlasting,** against **bronchitis.** Relieves **pulmonary congestion** and eliminates **irritative cough,** see **description of the plant.**

- **Mouse-ear hawkweed,** the infusion ingested it helps positively as **anticatarral, in case of respiratory and cold problems.** It is recommended **in bronchial treatment or bronchitis,** see **description of the plant.**

- **Myrrh,** ingested and in gargles is extremely useful **in catarrh,** and respiratory affections **in times of colds,** see **description of the plant.**

- **Myrtle,** only use **in older than 6 years.** The infusion against **bronchitis and pulmonary emphysema** due to its **expectorant properties.** It is beneficial **against cough, ingested or in inhalations.** The ingested **essential oil** is beneficial in **decongesting the airways and sinuses,** see **description of the plant,** forms of use **VI and VII.**

- **Narrow-leaf strap fern,** the infusions is an effective remedy to treat disorders of the respiratory system such as **bronchitis and cough,** see **description of the plant,** form of use **VII.**

- **Nettle,** is used **against hemoptysis** (expulsion of blood through the airways due to **bleeding in the lungs),** see **description of the plant.**

- **Niaouli,** used **only older than 6 years,** infusion ingested or in topical use (massages directly on the skin) to treat respiratory tract infections such **as bronchitis, cough.** Against **nasal congestion and sinusitis** pour on a handkerchief 2 drops of niaouli oil, 2 drops of lavender oil and 2 drops of eucalyptus oil. Breathe as many times as possible, see **description of the different plants,** for **bronchitis and cough,** see form of use **VII.**

- **Onion,** drink the resulting liquid by boiling it with a little honey **(only older than 1 year).** Due to its high content of vitamin C, it helps greatly to **cure the cold,** as well as **nasal and pectoral congestion.** The topical use of ½ onion during the night, closest to the head (bedside table), relieves and helps to breathe, improving the rest **in congestions, colds or respiratory ailments.** It turns black, it should be changed every two day at most, the drawback is the smell that comes off, you can also drink the boiled liquid afterwards, see **description of the plant and of the Honey.**

- **Orange,** allied in cooling and **colds both the consumption and the juice** and for the **states of congestion** in which we have no appetite and we look for something that hydrates and purifies us at the same time, see **description of the plant.**

- **Oregano,** the infusion ingested it helps **reduce** the symptoms of **bronchitis,** being very beneficial **against pulmonary emphysema.** It also helps reduce the symptoms of **catarrhs, colds and relieves cough.** It is a good remedy against **sinusitis,** see **description of the plant,** forms of use **IV and VII.**

- **Pansy,** the infusion ingested it is beneficial in cases of acute **bronchitis, lung problems, in catarrhs and colds, cough and whooping cough,** see **description of the plant.**

- **Paronychia plant,** the infusion ingested its used to treat **symptoms of bronchitis and colds,** see **description of the plant.**

- **Parsley,** increase their consumption in autumn or winter, in broths and soups, thanks to their qualities **against colds** (it does not help to avoid them, but it is useful to **alleviate their symptoms and shorten their duration),** see **description of the plant.**

- **Prunus,** the infusion of flowers, contribute to improve and cure **diseases of the lung and cough,** see **description of the plant.**

- **Quince,** it is very effective for treating **bronchial diseases,** in case of **colds and coughs,** see **description of the plant.**

- **Radish,** in **older than 3 years,** it is useful when fighting **against a cold,** see **description of the plant.**

- **Roselle plant,** because of its high vitamin C content, it **helps prevent cold** and other infectious diseases. If you **take when symptoms appear,** it will help much faster, see **description of the plant.**

- **Rowan,** the cooking ingested (even the dry fruits) fights and **relieves coughing,** see **description of the plant,** form of use **VII (1).**

- **Rye,** as daytime water due to its mucilages soothe situations of respiratory tract infections **such as colds,** softening **cough,** see **description of the plant,** form of use **VII.**

- **Safflower,** the infusion ingested of its flowers in Indian medicine is used for **chest pains** from congestion, **respiratory, pulmonary and pneumonic diseases, for expectorant cough,** see **description of the plant.**

- **Sage,** ingested can be **used from 6 years, never more than three daily infusions,** it's useful **against colds.** Inhaling a decoction of its leaves relieves **mild bronchial asthma.** It can also be used **for coughing up phlegm,** see **description of the plant.**

- **Sanicle,** la infusión ingerida se utiliza in case of **bronchitis, pulmonary emphysema,** and acts **against bronchiectasis,** see **description of the plant.**

- **Scots pine,** for respiratory problems such as **bronchitis, congestion, colds, sinusitis, coughs,** it is used in inhalations **(only over 6 years),** or you can rub your chest with your preparations in case of congestion. You can **also eat pine nuts (from small),** for the same purpose, see **description of the plant.**

- **Small-leaved lime,** the infusion ingested it is ideal **for colds and symptoms cough,** for the presence of mucilage, see **description of plant.**

- **Soursop,** used in any modality is expectorant, helps to treat diseases related to the respiratory system, **including bronchitis, colds, coughs,** see **description of the plant.**

- **Spearmint,** the infusion ingested, **from 6 years,** it is used in the **processes of colds** and expectorant that **relieves cough,** see **description of the plant.**

- **Tamarillo,** its consumption is good **in case of colds.** Controls **the rhinitis** by taking at least twice a day the juice of this fruit, see **description of plant.**

- **Tamarind,** the infusion ingested it is effective **against colds and coughs,** see **description of the plant,** form of use **VII.**

- **Tea of Aragon,** the infusion it is effective in treating respiratory tract infections, **such as colds, and coughing attacks,** see **description of plant.**

- **Thyme,** the infusion ingested it´s very effective for the **colds.** It has excellent expectorant properties, and moderate the **effects of cough and whooping cough.** It is very useful in cases of bronchitis, see **description of the plant.**

- **Tree lungwort,** the infusion it is indicated for **bronchitis, colds, powerful remedy against cough,** being of balsamic effect, see **description of the plant,** form of use **VII.**

- **Virginia water horehound,** the infusion ingested soothes the airways by eliminating irritation such as **excessive coughing and congestion,** see **description of the plant.**

- **Watermelon,** protects the **respiratory and pulmonary system,** see description of the plant.

- **West Indian cherry,** to fight **bronchial and respiratory infections** such as **sinusitis,** and to prevent **colds,** see **description of the plant.**

- **White Chilean myrtle,** being expectorant **relieves cough,** see description of the plant.

- **White clover,** for **catarrhal processes and colds,** see **description plant.**

- **Withe mulberry,** a syrup is made that is used for colds and catarrhs in the respiratory tract, see **description of the plant.**

- **White mustard,** it is used for its effectiveness in respiratory diseases, **bronchitis, pulmonary congestion, colds, cough,** see **description of plant.**

- **White nettle,** the infusion of flowers and flowery tips ingested and cooked, in **lung diseases,** see **description of plant,** forms of use **VII and VIII.**

- **Yellow trumpetbush,** the infusion is beneficial **against cough,** see **description of the plant.**

Skin/Cardinals - Diaper rash - Sweat/Odor

Never replace the medication by the natural remedies. These remedies are supported, **you should always consult with your child's doctor.**

- **Acanthus,** the external use of its juice, in poultices, as an anti-inflammatory is **effective for bruises,** see **description of the plant.**

- **Aloe vera,** its inner gel **cleans the skin** in depth. In **babies** it relieves **the irritation** caused **by diapers,** see **description of the plant.**

- **Broadleaf cattail,** the infusion in topical use relieves and improves **erysipelas and local inflammations** of the skin, see **description of plant.**

- **Common daisy,** for **the bruises,** see **description of the plant.**

- **Cornstarch,** it is used to **treat rashes** that occur **in babies by the use of diapers,** just rub a little of the product on the intimate areas before changing. **Also against excessive sweating** which can be very unpleasant because of **the bad smell** it generates. It is **recommended to rub the armpits** with a cotton dipped in alcohol and then with a little bit of cornstarch, see **description of the plant Corn and of the Cornstarch.**

- **Durmast oak,** for **the chilblains** boil 30 gr. of its crust and 40 gr. of field horsetail in 1 liter of water 10 minutes. Rest and make warm baths in the affected areas, see **description of the different plants.**

- **Ginger,** very beneficial **to treat inflamed skin and bruises.** No need to peel, wash very well crush and apply on the bruise inflamed and hold with a bandage and keep it as long as possible. **For a better and faster result,** put the ginger on the skin during the night combined with a cold compress, **will removes bruises and haematomas** from the body, see **description of the plant.**

- **Great mullein,** the leaves lightly boiled on **the skin** or in ointments, **favors the bruises,** having it a while on them, see **description of the plant.**

- **Hamamelis virginiana,** its water is excellent **in topical use to cardinals,** maintain 3 minutes, 3 times daily, see **description of the plant,** form of use **VII (2).**

- **Heath speedwell,** by poultices, washes, dressings **to soften dry skin from the cold,** see **description of the plant.**

- **Henna tree,** the leaves diluted in water are used against **the stench of the feet,** see **description of the plant.**

- **Lettuce,** to reduce the **sweat and odor of the armpits and feet,** apply your juice, see **description of the plant.**

- **Marjoram,** its used in topical use mixed with honey **to improve the cardinals,** see **description of the plant.**

- **Marsh mallow,** its uses **root extracts** to **reduce chilblains** in the swelling **of the hands and feet** due to **excessive cold,** see **description of the plant.**

- **Mint,** the infusion **in topical use** on the skin, it generates a sensation of freshness **against sweat,** and of local relaxation **as a sedative,** see **description of the plant.**

- **Pansy,** the infusion in topical use to treat **rashes like hives.** It has ideal antimicrobial properties for the treatment of **skin problems such as diaper rash,** see **description of the plant.**

- **Parsley,** apply at regular intervals **in the area of the bruise** to reduce inflammation until the skin returns to its normal temperature and color, see **description of the plant.**

- **Patchouli,** just **two or three drops** on a cotton ball, rub in the armpits **to avoid body odor,** see **description of the plant.**

- **Rooibos,** the infusion in topical use it is especially useful **in hives and diaper rashes**, through washing and dressing, see **description of the plant.**

- **Sage,** the infusion **in topical use** controls **excess sweating** and **bad body odor,** see **description of the plant.**

- **Sanicle,** the infusion ingested and in topical use it acts on exanthems **(rash of measles, rubella, chicken pox, scarlet fever, dengue or typhus),** see **description of the plant.**

- **Solomon's seal,** it is applied in the form of a poultice, **against ecchymosis or cardinals,** see **description of the plant.**

- **Yarrow,** the infusion ingested or in topical use improves the appearance of **the cardinals,** see **description of the plant,** form of use **VII.**

- **Yellow sweet clover,** its used in topical use to superficial **bruises,** see description of the plant.

- **Yellow trumpetbush,** the infusion in topical use its used to cure smallpox, sores or symptoms of hives, see **description of the plant.**

Vegetations / Adenoids

Never replace the medication by the natural remedies. These remedies are supported, **you should always consult with your child's doctor**.

- **Elder,** see in **Tea tree,** see **the different descriptions of the plants.**

- **Eucalyptus,** see in **Tea tree,** see **the different descriptions of the plants.**

- **Garlic,** to consume in prevention of **vegetations,** see **description plant.**

- **Honey,** it acts against vegetations by being an effective anti-inflammatory and antibacterial agent. It is advisable to add some drops of lemon juice to a teaspoon of honey **(from 1 year)** and take 2 to 3 times a day. Daily helps to reduce swollen adenoids and can even treat symptoms such as pain and burning, see **the different descriptions of the plants and of the Honey.**

- **Lemon,** see **in Honey,** see **the different descriptions of the plants.**

- **Tea tree,** for the vegetations, the inhalation of Eucalyptus, Elder flowers, and essence of the Tea tree, in 2 or 3 drops, it is very effective, after two weeks you can see the results, see **the different descriptions of the plants.**

Wounds - Blisters

Never replace the medication by the natural remedies. These remedies are supported, **you should always consult with your child's doctor**.

- **Ajuga iva,** the infusion in topical use applied **in the form of washes or dressings,** for superficial **wounds,** see **description of the plant.**

- **Apple,** in topical use through the poultice of an apple mush used **to heal wounds,** see **description of the plant.**

- **Breckland thyme,** the infusion **in topical use** its used, through washes and dressings **to heal wounds,** see **description of the plant.**

- **Broadleaf plantain,** heat the leaves to put on poultices, their properties **cure and relieve** inflammations and **stops bleeding from the wounds. Skin ulcers** are relieved by washing or dressings, see **description of the plant.**

- **Brussels sprout,** it is used **to heal old wounds,** wash first with hot water and then apply very crushed cabbage (directly on the skin, with a cotton gauze or similar). **In recent wounds** it is advisable to simply put just a few cabbage leaves directly for half an hour, see **description of the plant.**

- **Carrot,** place **on the blisters,** grated carrot by poultice, see **description of the plant.**

- **Chamomile,** the infusion in topical use its used against **blisters,** and scarring of **cuts or wounds,** see **description of the plant.**

- **Chilean myrtle,** the crust with leaves, through washing is used **for wounds,** see **description of the plant,** form of use **VII.**

- **Clary sage,** in topical use to moderate and calm inflammations, **relieve abscesses, swellings and wounds,** see **description of the plant,** forms of use **VII (8 and 9).**

- **Common fleabane,** the infusion in topical use its used to **the wounds** (in washes and dressings), see **description of the plant.**

- **Cornstarch,** to avoid **an infection if the blisters burst,** apply a paste of cornstarch and honey **(from 1 year).** Also its used to treat **small wounds** with antiseptic and healing properties, see **description of the Corn plant, Cornstarch and of the Honey.**

- **Durmast oak,** the infusion in topical use it is an astringent remedy, in washes to dressings **against fissures of the anus, to heal slow healing wounds, eczema, burns, chilblains,** see **description plant,** form of use **VII.**

- **Dyer's greenweed,** the infusion **in topical use** through washes and dressings, heals and relieves **wounds,** see **description of the plant.**

- **Echinacea,** it is sufficient to dilute 5 drops of your tincture in half a teaspoon (of dessert) of water and impregnate a dressing and apply directly **on the blister,** see **description of the plant.**

- **Eggshell,** use as a bandage the inner part of the eggshell, has a thin transparent film very useful **to heal cuts and scratches,** see **description of the plant.**

- **Elms,** the infusion in topical use, as washes, disinfects and heals **wounds,** see **description of the plant,** form of use **VII.**

- **English primrose,** the infusion in topical use in the form of baths, or washes for **oozing wounds,** see **description of the plant.**

- **European searocket,** the juice is an effective remedy **as a wound healing,** see **description of the plant.**

- **Garlic,** its used the juice of 2 or 3 cloves of garlic directly **on the blisters,** see **description of the plant.**

- **Grapevine,** suck the powder obtained by crushing dried leaves as astringent and coagulant **to stop nosebleeds or epistaxis.** Also to stop bleeding **from wounds,** spread powder over them, see **description plant.**

- **Heath speedwell,** the infusion its used by poultice, for the healing **of sores and wounds,** see **description of the plant.**

- **Herb Bennet,** in topical use, see **description of plant,** form of use **IV.**

- **Honey,** for the **blisters** use a mixture of equal parts of honey **(from 1 year)** and wheat germ oil, apply in the area to reduce friction or irritation that may exist see **description of the plant and of the Honey.**

- **Horehound,** the infusion **in topical use** its used in **infected or badly healed wounds** through washes and dressings, see **description of plant.**

- **Marjoram,** the infusion **in topical use,** through washes and dressings, soothes and heals **minor wounds,** see **description of the plant.**

- **Marsh mallow,** the infusion of **the leaves and roots,** through washing is used to clean and heal **small wounds,** see **description of the plant.**

- **Mouse-ear hawkweed,** the infusion ingested or in topical use **being coagulant** it can be used as an antihemorrhagic **in case of nosebleed,** see **description of the plant.**

- **Myrrh,** the infusion or the oil in topical use it is a refreshing action **for blisters,** also helps to heal and disinfect **wounds, sores** and **skin ulcers,** see **description of the plant.**

- **Myrtle,** the liquefaction and its oil are used as antiseptic in topical use to clean **wounds, sores and boils** on the skin, see **description of the plant,** forms of use **VI and IX.**

- **Onion,** drink the resulting liquid by boiling it with a little honey **(only older than 1 year),** it is used **for internal wounds,** see **description of the plant and of the Honey.**

- **Oregano,** its used through washes and dressings, **disinfects and heals wounds,** see **description of the plant,** form of use **IV.**

- **Pansy,** the infusion in topical use through washes and dressings, its used to **superficial wounds,** see **description of the plant.**

- **Papaya,** its consumption **from 3 years,** it helps the **coagulation of internal and external wounds,** for its fibrin content, easily assimilable and valuable substance, see **description of the plant.**

- **Patchouli,** in topical use diluted in another oil is used to treat **to heal wounds** and helps to **soothe** inflammation or irritation, see **description of the plant.**

- **Psoralea,** the infusion or the poultice is used to heal **sores and wounds,** see **description of the plant,** forms of use **IV and VII.**

- **Rowan,** cooking and tincture in topical use is used **to heal wounds,** see **description of the plant,** forms of use **VII (1).**

- **Sage,** the infusion in through washes and dressings as a **wound healing,** see **description of the plant.**

- **Sanicle,** the infusion **in topical use** its used through washes and dressings **to the wounds,** see **description of the plant.**

- **Sowthistle,** the broth of the leaves in topical use for the treatment of **hemorrhages in wounds,** see **description of plant,** form of consume **VIII.**

- **Spiked loosestrife,** the infusion in washes to **heal wounds,** see **description of the plant.**

- **Tansy,** the infusion as anti-inflammatory and healing **for wounds.** Boil 30 gr. of flowers and stems in 1 liter of water. Cover and use in washes or dressings after resting, see **description of the plant.**

- **Tea of Aragon,** the infusion in topical use cleans **the wounds,** see **description of the plant.**

- **Tea tree,** in topical use apply with a cotton ball mixed with water **on the blisters** twice a day, in order to calm the pain and prevent infection, see **description of the plant.**

- **Thyme,** the infusion in topical use it is very useful to **close, to scar and heal wounds,** see **description of the plant.**

- **Tomato,** to **heal wounds** is used in the form of a poultice, see **description of the plant.**

- **Verdolaga,** the infusion by poultice or dressing for **the wounds.** Also the flowering tops as antihemorrhagic, see **description of the plant.**

- **Walnut tree,** the infusion of the leaves in topical use as washes or dressings, for **oozing wounds,** see **description of the plant,** form of use **VII.**

- **Wheat,** for **the blisters** a mixture of **equal parts of honey and wheat germ oil** is used **(from 1 year),** apply in the area to reduce friction or irritation that could exist. Contains selenium, an antioxidant that protects cells, zinc contributes **to the healing of wounds,** see **description of the plant and of the Honey.**

- **White nettle,** the infusion and powder is beneficial to cure hemorrhages as a **good coagulant in wounds,** see **description of the plant,** form of use **VII.**

Sweeteners

The **glucose** is one of the main ingredients that brings **more energy** to our body.

During **childhood,** consumption is very important as it plays a fundamental role in **the development of tissues.** The brain absorbs 20% of the glucose that is ingested, nourishes **the nervous system serving** for a perfect **physical and mental development.** Its consumption replenishes **glycogen deposits in muscles and liver.** It helps to **conciliate the sleep** thanks to its relaxing effect.

Its lack increases the appetite and **can produce anxiety,** being necessary a daily dose of glucose either in pastry or fruit, but with **moderate consumption** to avoid other problems due to excess intake. There are sweeteners or syrups of different medicinal plants, choose the highest purity and **to avoid caries problems** it is advisable to **use only a few drops,** given its concentration in sugars is very high. Low-glycemic sweeteners **of less than 5%** are recommended **in children, also ...Continue on next page**

... for diabetics, with diets or cholesterol problems, preferably **0.2% Birch sugar** or **Stevia, without any sugar,** although with a slight licorice flavor. **The little** ones are often **reluctant to drink infusions, because of their taste,** but they can be masked with Mint, a drop of Vanilla or any sweetener pleasant to your palate (see possible contraindications or interactions).

- **Acer,** excellent sweetener is the use of its honey (also known as Maple syrup) syrup extracted by the evaporation of the sap of the tree, contains a large amount of sugars simple and only 0.7% minerals. **Contraindicated for diabetics and persons intolerant to glucose,** see **description of plant.**

- **Apple,** there is a syrup of the apple ideal for the little ones, and with more food than refined sugar, it serves to vary the taste of any medicine or drink that should taken, see **description of the plant.**

- **Barley,** the molasses is obtained equal and with the same benefit as that of rice as sweetener. It is undoubtedly a good substitute for white sugar (completely devoid of nutrients), **especially for children,** see **description of the plant.**

- **Birch,** there is a hypoglycaemic sugar, with 0.2 gr. of sugar, very interesting for diabetics or diets, see **description of the plant.**

- **Blue agave,** With its it is possible a syrup that serves as a sweetener. There are different preparations being extremely sweet using only a few drops, being able to find one of low glycemic power, ideal for minors, persons with diets and diabetics, see **description of the plant.**

- **Coconut,** there is a sugar **the** coconut, see **description of the plant.**

- **Honey,** the honey can contain up to 150 different elements in its composition, very natural and delicious sweetener, but should be consumed in moderation, **only over 1 year,** see **description of the Honey.**

- **Larch tree,** in summer the leaves sweat a liquid that is used to sweeten, beneficial for persons with diabetes, see **description of the plant.**

- **Onion,** you can make onion molasses as a sweetener, it is obtained just like rice by decoction. It is a good substitute for white sugar (completely devoid of nutrients), **especially for children,** see **description of the plant.**

- **Polypodium fern,** the flavor of the root is sweet (contain sucrose), it can be used without any inconvenience as a sweetener. **It exists in powder form. Diabetics should consult the doctor or specialist,** see **description of the plant.**

- **Pryckli pear,** there is a sugar **the** pryckli pear, and an ideal sweetener molasses for diets containing 67% less calories than sugar. **Diabetics,** better to consult about different preparations, see **description of plant.**

- **Rice,** as a molasses is used as a sweetener, as it is a fermented product, its digestibility is greater, and it contains, just like whole cane sugar integral, a certain amount of vitamins and minerals from these cereals. Also, if they have been elaborated with temperatures below 70º C, they contain enzymatic properties so it is important to obtain them of good quality. Sweeten something less than sugar and they are quite soft on the palate. It is certainly a **good substitute for white sugar** (completely devoid of nutrients), especially for the child population. There is a **rice syrup** in the market, see **description of the plant.**

- **Stevia,** used as a sweetener is ideal against tooth decay and for diabetics as it does not contain sugar, being important in any diet due to its low calorie content, see **description of the plant.**

- **Strawberries,** there is a syrup of the strawberries ideal for the little ones, and with more food than refined sugar, it serves to vary the taste of any medicine or drink that should taken, see **description of the plant.**

- **Sugarcane,** the cane sugar integral, it is one of the sweeteners richest in vitamins and minerals. **Consider that even the excess of this sugar is detrimental to the dental health.** Varies the conditions **when used in juice,** it is important to consume the juice as soon as it is extracted, it tends to oxidize in 15 minutes. The sugar is obtained by evaporating the cane juice by heating or lyophilization, **of all types of sugar is the healthiest, because contains some minerals and vitamins when the artisanal manufacturing process is respected.**

The real integral cane sugar is not brown, but it has a slightly toasted color and cakes easily on contact with moisture. **We will find it in stores specializing in biological products.** The one that is usually sold in hypermarkets is full of additives, it has nothing to do with the real thing. Neither the colour, nor the texture, nor its properties, nor the process of industrial production. There is also **cane molasses,** in specialized stores. **Contraindicated for diabetics and persons intolerant to the glucose,** see **description of the plant,** form of use **X.**

Forms of use of plants letters A - B

- **Agrimony,** see **description of the plant.**
  - **VII - The infusion it is made** boiling 100 gr. of dried leaves and flowers in a liter of water, rest and use, sweeten to taste.

- **Almond,** see **description of the plant.**
  - **VI - It acts** effectively **as a laxative,** providing **a child** with two tablespoons of almond oil **on an empty stomach.**

- **Amaranth,** see **description of the plant.**
  - **VIII - There are different ways** to prepare it being very easy to add and consume. Roasted grains or flour. Prepare a tasty salad with its leaves, or use them as a filling for pastries, cakes or all kinds of dishes.

- Anacahuita, see **description of the plant.**

- **VII - The infusion it is made** boiling 20 gr. per liter of water, drink hot 4 or 5 times a day, sweeten to taste.

- Baccharises, see **description of the plant and of the Honey.**

- **VII (1) -** The infusion is made by boiling 1 liter of water and adding a spoonful of Baccharises. Let boil 15 minutes more. Rest 5 minutes covered. Strain and drink warm two cups daily (on an empty stomach and before sleep), sweeten preferably with Honey **(over 1 year).**

- Barley, see **description of the different plants.**

- **VII - The decoction is made** with crushed Barley (semolina preferably). Boil 40-50 gr. according to desired density, with semolina less quantity, for 10 minutes in 1 ½ liter of water with a Cinnamon stick. Once it starts to boil, put on a low heat until 1 liter approx. Strain and use, **you can drink it as day water,** even **for baby bottles** mixed in juice or directly. The barley left in the colander can be used with yoghurts, in salads, baby porridge. **Also raw crushed barley** can be added to any stew and cook in turn **as a vitamin supplement.**

- Bistort, see **description of the plant.**

- **VII - The infusion its made** pouring 35 gr. of the rhizome (tuber from which the roots or the stem of the flowers come out) per liter of boiling water. Keep 5 minutes, strain and use. For mouth or throat problems, in rinses or gargles, **without sweetening.** To prevent stomach upsets such as diarrhea, stomatitis and urethritis, drink three cups a day, sweetening to taste.
- **IX - The concentrated liquefaction its made** by pouring 75 gr. of rhizome into 1 liter of boiling water. Heat 15 minutes more over a low heat for gargle in cases of pharyngitis and canker sores, **without sweetening.**

- Bitter wood, see **description of the plant.**

- **IX - The liquefaction its made** using between 5 and 10 gr. of crust and / or wood per liter of water, **drink a cup before each meal.**

- **Blackberry,** see **description of the plant.**
  - **VIII - Use their fruits,** and squeeze them as much as possible by collecting the juice and adding sugar (double the weight of the juice) or **sweetener** to taste. **Heat over low heat** until they reach the consistency of a syrup. Cool completely and pack in bottles, keep tightly closed. **To use,** dilute two tablespoons of dessert in a glass of warm water, and **practice gargle** when the throat is red or swollen.

- **Bloodroot,** see **description of the plant.**
  - **The infusion its made** placing in a cup with boiling water some leaves of the plant. Drink hot
  - **Another infusion its made** with 20 gr. of the plant in 1 liter of water. Drink hot three times a day.
  - **In washes, rinses or gargles,** boil 1 liter of water 10 minutes with 50 gr. of the plant, **without sweetening.**

- **Broadleaf plantain,** see **description of the plant.**
  - **VII - The infusion its made** boiling water in a cup, pour a spoonful of green or dry leaves, cover and stand for 10 minutes, strain, and drink. **In mouthwashes or gargles, without sweetening.**
  - **IX - The liquefaction its made** in a cup of cold water 2 tablespoons chopped leaves, liquefy very well, strain and take on an empty stomach, **very useful for stomach ulcers, gastritis and irritable bowel.**

Forms of use of plants letters C - D - E

- **Calamus,** see **description of the plant.**
  - **VII - The infusion its prepared** with a small spoonful of roots soaking overnight at ¼ litre of cold water. The next day it is heated in a bainmarie and strained for a warm drink, sweetened to taste.
  - **IX - The liquefaction its made** cleaning the fresh roots and liquefy before they dry, drink what you want, sweeten to taste.

- **Cecropia,** see **description of the plant.**
  - **VII - The infusion it is made** pouring 20 gr. of leaves per liter of boiling water, boil 10 minutes more. Rest and strain, you can drink up to 3 cups. **It is recommended** to sweeten it to be very bitter.

- **Chachacoma,** see **description of the plant and of the Honey.**
  - **VII - The infusion its made** boiling 20 gr. in 1 liter of water for 10 minutes, strain and drink 3 cups a day. **It is power with honey (in older than 1 year),** or sweetened to taste.

- **Chestnut fruit,** see **description of the plant.**
  - **VIII - Food very high in fiber,** it is recommended **as a mild laxative.** Also, being **dual property** in cases of **mild diarrhea,** this fiber will make it go back to its natural state. It is recommended as a treatment for those who have **intestinal problems,** allowing bowel movements to be much more regular.

- **Chestnut tree,** see **description of the plant.**
  - **VII (1) - The infusion ingested its made** with 60 gr. of leaves or crust per liter of water. Boil 15 minutes. Strain and drink 3 - 4 cups daily.
  - **VII (3) - The infusion in gargles and rinses its made** pouring a handful of tender leaves or half a handful of dry leaves per litre of wáter. Boil, strain and let stand to use twice a day, **without sweetening.**

- **Chickpea,** see **description of the plant.**
  - **VIII - Legume of great richness in fiber** that acts favorably in maintaining the **intestine** with good activity, favoring the intestinal transit **as a laxative.**

- **Chilean myrtle,** see **description of the plant.**
  - **The decoction for** the intestine and **dysentery is,** using the crust and a handful of leaves in 1 liter of water for 15 minutes and drinking. **In topical use** of lavatories, gargle or rinses, **without sweetening.**
  - **The cooking of roots,** being astringent, is used **for the intestine.**

- **Clary sage,** see **description of the different plants.**
  - **VII (4) - Sore throat,** mix in 950 milliliters of hot water, 2 drops of Cranesbills oil, 2 drops of Clary sage oil and 1 drop of Indian sandalwood oil. Impregnate a cloth with this preparation and place as a compress, in the neck and throat several times a day.
  - **VII (7) - For the problems of asthmatics** the essential oil inhaled helps **to calm the spasms,** and the tightness of the muscles that surround **the bronchi.**
  - **VII (8) - The infusion its leaves in topical use,** relieves **respiratory respiratory from the cold,** and **stomach problems, without sweetening.**
  - **VII (9) - In topical use,** using **1 drop** of essential oil is sufficient.

- **Cornflower,** see **description of the plant.**
  - **VII - The infusion it is made** by boiling water and adding a teaspoon of dessert, with petals and leaves. Rest, strain and drink warm 2 or 3 cups a day, sweeten to taste. **In topical** use, **without sweetening.**

- **Cowslip primrose,** see **description of the plant.**
  - **VII - The infusion its made** with 60 gr. per liter of water. Boil, filter, rest for a few minutes. Drink 2 cups daily or gargle several times a day (no more than 4), **without sweetening.**

- **Durmast oak,** see **description of the different plants.**
  - **The infusion its made** boiling a glass of water. Pour 1 teaspoon of crust, washed, bring to a boil 15 minutes more. Rest, strain and drink.
  - **The infusion for the chilblains,** boil 30 gr. of its crust and 40 gr. of Field horsetail in 1 liter of water 10 minutes. Rest and make warm baths in the affected areas, **without sweetening.**

- **Elms,** see **description of the plant.**
  - **VII - The infusion its prepared** with 2 teaspoons of crust per liter of water. Boil, strain and drink. **Used** in topical use, **without sweetening.**

- Erythraea chilensis, see **description of plant.**

- **VII - It is used macerating** a handful of the plant in cold water for several hours, on an empty stomach take 1 large spoonful, although it is effective in less time taking from 3 to 5 in the day.
- **VII - As day water:** add a portion of root previously washed, chopped and crushed in a liter of water. Boil until the liquid is reduced by half to drink.
- **VII - Preparation of infusions:** use 20 gr. of the rhizome or root in half a liter of boiling water, drink hot.

Forms of use of plants letters F - G - H

- Fennel, see **description of the different plants.**

- **The infusion in gargles** of Fennel, Mint, Sage **(from 6 years old)** and Valerian, against **blockage of the throat** causing sleep apnea, **insomnia** and hoarseness, **without sweetening.**
- **Another simpler option** is to boil water and at rest add 2 teaspoons of your crushed seeds a little, rest for 10 minutes. Strain and drink ½ h. before each meal.

- Fenugreek, see **description of the plants.**

- **VII - The decoctions or infusions**, having an **unpleasant odor, is used in a very small quantities or** mixed with other aromatic herbs. **More than 100 gr. per day can cause diarrhea and nausea.**
- **VIII - It can be consumed** directly as a complement to salad and fish, **of unpleasant odor** in the diet **is used in a very small quantities** or mixed with other aromatic herbs, Turmeric, Curry or in fish in papillote. **More than 100 gr. per day can cause diarrhea and nausea.**

- Garden nasturtium, see **description of the plant.**

- **The infusion its made** with a small spoonful for each cup of boiling water. Drink between 2 and 3 cups a day before meals. **In topical use, without sweetening.** **...Continue on next page**

...

- **The decoction is made** with 50 gr. per liter of boiling water. Rest 15 minutes, strain and drink a cup twice a day. **In topical use, without sweetening.**

- Geranium or Cranesbills, see **description of the different plants.**

- • **The infusion its made** with 4 gr. of root in 100 ml of water, it can be accompanied with infusions of Chamomile, Spearmint, Mint. For mouth and throat conditions, it is recommended every 4 hours, gargling **without sweetening.**

- Hazel, see **description of the plant.**

- **VII - The infusion it is made** boiling 25 gr. of leaves per liter of water, leave 10 minutes, **rest and drink.**

- Herb Bennet, see **description of the plant.**

- **IV - It is used** when boiling between 60 - 90 gr. of root in a liter of water, or something less if the root is dry, for use in washes, dressings or plasters, **without sweetening.**
- **VII (1) - The infusion its made** boiling between 60 - 90 gr. of root in a liter of wáter, or something less weight if the root is dry. Drink 3 to 4 cups during the day.
- **VII (2) - For the throat the infusion its made** boiling between 60 - 90 gr. of root in a liter of water, or something less weight if the root is dry. Drink 3 to 4 cups during the day. It is also used in gargles, **without sweetening.**
- **VII (4) - For gastrointestinal disorders,** 250 gr. of boiling water are poured in 2 tablespoons of root of the plant, rest ¼ of hour. Strain and drink 2 to 3 cups daily.

- Honeysuckle, see **description of the different plants.**

- **The infusion (of the white flower)** is used for respiratory tract infections **in colds,** it is an excellent complement mix with Ginger (mucolytic and anti-inflammatory). Also the syrup reached **...Continue**

... the acute stage of the process It has excellent antiseptic and balsamic properties **for cough and throat** in its various ailments.

- **The infusion (of the white flower)** is used with effectiveness in **intestinal dysentery.**
- **The infusion** of the crust for inflammations of the ganglia.

- Hops, see **description of the plant.**

- **The infusion of the flowers** is made with 25 gr. of flowers in a liter of water. Boil for 10 minutes. Strain and drink up to 3 times a day.
- **The infusion of the grain,** boil 15 gr. in ½ liter of water. You should drink a cup on an empty stomach.

- Horsetail, see **description of the plant.**

- **The infusion ingested** its prepared with 15 gr. of dry leaves, boil in 1 liter of water for 2-5 minutes. Rest, filter with a clean cloth and drink 4 cups of 250 ml., **only for one day.**
- **The infusion in topical use** its made boiling 5 gr. of the plant in 1 liter of water 2 minutes. Rest, filter and store in a container. Use in gargles, washed or baths of seat to reduce inflammations, **without sweetening.**

Forms of use of plants letters I - L - M

- Iceland moss, see **description of the plant.**

- **Infusion as a aperitif tonic,** is made with 15 gr. of the stem added to 1 liter of boiled water, rest 10 minutes and drink.
- **Double decoction,** used **to eliminate bitter substances,** boil 15 gr. of the stem in 1 liter of water for 1 minute, wash thoroughly afterwards. Return to cook in 1 ½ liter, with another water for ½ hour, rest and drink.

- Linden tree, see **description of the plant.**
- **VII - The infusion it is made** when boiling a cup of water with a handful of flowers of the tree or about 6 leaves in its defect. Rest 5 minutes, strain and drink. In inhalations, rinses or gargles, **without sweetening.**

- Lungwort, see **description of the plant and of the honey.**
- **For the decoction** 80 gr. is recommended. per liter of water. Boil for 10 minutes, strain and **drink very hot** 4 or 5 cups a day. **To potentiate its effects** sweeten with honey **(over 1 year).**

- Myrtle, see **description of the plant.**
- **VI - Use the essence** of 1 to 2 drops three times a day, before the main meals.
- **VII - The infusion its made** with a teaspoon of leaves per-cup of water. Also with 15 gr. of leaves per liter of water.
- **IX - The liquefaction its made** boiling 20 gr. of leaves per liter of water for 5 minutes. By means of washes or dressings, **without sweetening.**

Forms of use of plants letters N - O

- Narrow-leaf strap fern, see **description of the plant**
- **VII - As day water** add a portion of root previously washed, chopped and crushed in a liter of water. Boil until the liquid is reduced by half, drink sweetening to taste.

- Niaouli, see **description of the different plants.**
- **To use pour** 2 drops of niaouli essential oil in an infusion of Thyme and drink. Used in topical use, **without sweetening.**

- Oats, see **description of the different plants.**
- **For use in children under 1 year, better semolina,** from the year can be added to your crushed oatmeal porridges, **sometimes raw, repudiate it,** in which case boil the semolina that is sold, and mix it with your porridge, even the liquid can be mixed with **...Continue**

... the juices. For adults boil oatmeal and use in yoghurts, meals, salads, the liquid can be drunk as day water with a little Cinnamon, it can also be sweetened to taste.

- **Oregano,** see **description of the plant.**
  - **IV - In topical use** boil for 10 minutes 50 gr. per liter of water and used in lotions, **gargles,** mouthwashes **compresses** or dressings, **without sweetening.**
  - **VII - The infusion its made** with one tablespoon of dessert per-cup. Boil for 10 minutes, strain and drink 3 times a day, before or after meals.

Forms of use of plants letter P

- **Papaya,** see **description of the plant.**
  - **VII - Against the pinworms** you can make an infusion with your seeds, **sweeten to taste, are very bitter.**

- **Perforate St John's-wort,** see **description of the plant.**
  - **VII (1) - The infusion its made** when boiling parts of the plant for 3 minutes. Rest 5 minutes, strain and drink 2 to 3 cups daily. **In** gargles, **without sweetening.**

- **Pineapple,** see **description of different plants.**
  - **IX -** To **peel and boil the pineapple rinds or peels** with a cinnamon stick in 1 ½ of water, until 1 liter remains. Drink cold on an empty stomach, **as a laxative** it is effective almost immediately in some persons, the rest take during the day. To eat the peeled fruit and do not bite in the mouth (usually occurs if it is not very ripe), it is recommended to soak with salt between 5 and 10 minutes.

- **Pollen,** see **description of the Pollen.**
  - **It is recommended to take pollen** for 20 days, and rest for 10 days, and continue for the recovery of health and vigor.

...Continue on next page

...

- **VIII (2) - Children between 3 and 5 years,** a little less than a spoonful (12 gr.)
- **VIII (3) - Children between 6 y 12 years,** a   little more thanone teaspoon tureen rasa (16 gr.)

- Pomegranate, see **description of the plants and of the Honey.**

- **Preferably consumed on an empty stomach,** to extract the seeds simply to cut it in half and hit the part of the shell with a spoon. It can also be cut in four quarters to go taking off the seeds more easily.
- **You can make juice** with its seeds or use the commercialized one, better to sweeten with Stevia or Honey. The juice leaves a slightly harsh feeling on the tongue, for the tannins, of astringent property. It can be mixed with apple, orange, carrot, ginger. **Persons with constipation should not abuse pomegranate juice.**

- Prunus, see **description of the different plants and the Honey.**

- **VIII - For habitual constipation** mix well 30 gr. of fresh plum pulp, 10 gr. of berries of Elder, 5 gr. of Cream of tartar, and 5 gr. of the leaves of Senna. Carefully chop and mix, add as much honey to the mixture as desired to obtain a dense paste, keep the preparation in a glass jar. Take 20 to 30 gr. daily **to regularize the intestine.**

- Psoralea, see **description of the plant.**

- **IV - With dry powdered leaves** sprinkle the wound, covered with gauze for 24 h. prevents it from becoming infected and prevents the formation of pus and, accelerating healing and faster cure.
- **VII - The infusion its prepared** with 30 gr. of leaves per ½ litre of water, boil for 30 minutes. Rest for a few minutes and use. **In washes,** rinses or gargles, **without sweetening.**

Forms of use of plants letters R - S

- **Rowan,** see **description of the plant.**
  - **VII (1) - The cooking its made** by pouring 1 tablespoon of the nuts into a glass of boiled water, keep on a low heat for 10 minutes, strain and drink 50 ml 3 times a day. Used in topical use, **without sweetening.**
  - **VII (2) - The juice, is made** with fresh berries washed and in a glass of boiled water take 1 tablespoon of the fruits, keep 10 minutes on low heat. Drink twice a day.

- **Rye,** see **description of the plant.**
  - **VII - It should be cooked** between 50 and 60 gr. of grain per liter of water, with semolina less quantity, until it is reduced by half. Drink in small sips throughout the day.
  - **VIII - To consume,** wash the grains 2 or 3 times, changing water, and leave it to soak for 8 to 12 h. Cook in water in proportion of 1 part rye per4 water, over medium heat for 1 ½ hours. Add to salads, rice, stews, etc.

- **Sowthistle,** see **description of the plant.**
  - **VIII - Tender leaves** are appetizing raw, in salad or cooked like spinach, can be **used as an ingredient** for the preparation of vegetable stews, and soups, being an excellent broth. **The roots** in cooking also act **against fever.** Both **the broth of the leaves** and the **cooking of the roots** is feasible to use **for washes or plasters.**

- **Spiny restharrow,** see **description of the plant.**
  - **VII - The infusion for rinsings or gargles,** is prepared with 3 gr. of root, boil for 10 minutes with a glass of water and half a vinegar, use **without sweetening.**

- **Strawberry plant,** see **description of the plant.**
  - **VII - The infusion its prepared** with two teaspoons of dessert of leaves for rinses or poultices, **without sweetening.**

...Continue on next page

... If it is **ingested** drink three times a day sweetening to taste. **The roots are prepared** with a teaspoon and are used in the same way.

- Sugarcane, see **description of the plant.**
- **IX - The juice or liquefaction is made** by boiling 30 gr. of cane root crumbled in ½ liter of water for 25 minutes, strain and use.

Forms of use of plants letters T - W - Z

- Tamarind, see **description of the plant.**
- **The infusion its made** with 10 grams of pulp per ½ liter of water. Boil the water, add the pulp and boil for 10 minutes. Turn off, rest and drin klukewarm on an empty stomach.
- **The infusion for babies or small children** uses the pulp and leaves for digestive problems or **constipation.** Reduced. As daytime water, **without sweetening,** it has depurative effects.
- **In case of indigestión or dysentery,** you can drink tamarind water by dissolving 40 gr. of pulp in a liter of boiling water. Boil for 5 minutes and add, if possible, some leaves. Turn off and let stand until cool. Drinking during the day. **Also** it is very useful to **fight the cases of vomiting.**

- Tree lungwort, see **description of the plant.**
- **VII - The infusion its made** bringing to boil about 30 gr. of the plant per liter of water. Boil 20 minutes, rest and filter. **Drink at maximum 3 cups a day,** very hot. **It can be enhanced** with other similar plants.

- Walnut tree, see **description of the plant.**
- **VII - The infusion its made** when boiling water and add their leaves, let boil 1 minute more. Rest for 5 minutes and drink 2 to 3 cups a day. **Used in** rinses or gargles, **without sweetening.**

- White nettle, see **description of the different plants and Honey.**

- **VII - The infusion its made** with two teaspoons of leaves, flowers or roots, separately or jointly, in 250 ml. of water. Boil, rest 5 minutes. Strain and drink. Take a cup 2 to 3 times a day.

- **VII - In topical use without sweetening,** the infusion of flowers and flowery tips in washes is beneficial to cure hemorrhages it is **a good coagulant for wounds. Also use the powder** on the wounds (3 gr. a day of dried flowers, with honey).

- **VIII - To consume** it can be used in soup and broths, prepared as spinach and other vegetables. Crushed boiled with garlic and oil, well crushed, for a bright green rice (vegetarian). Along with aromatic herbs in roasts, stews, game dishes.

Descriptions of plants letter A

- **Acanthus**
- **Acer**
- **Achiote tree, see Annato tree**
- **Acorn**
- **Agar Agar**
- **African myrrh, see Myrrh**
- **Agrimony**
- **Ajuga iva**
- **Allspice, see Jamaica pepper**
- **Almond**
- **Aloe vera**
- **Amaranth**
- **Anacahuita**
- **Annato tree**
- **Apple**
- **Arugula, see Roquet**
- **Asafoetida**
- **Ash**
- **Azuki red beans**

- Acanthus, (Acanto, en español)

"Acanthus mollis", also know as Bear's breeches of origin mediterranean, from Portugal and northwest Africa to eastern Croatia. Perennial plant with small flowers of unpleasant aroma. The leaves and root are used in infusion. **It has a low level of toxicity, in some persons it generates allergy** and skin contact irritation.   **...Continue on next page**

... **The infusion ingested** it can cause **diarrhea. Contraindicated ingested in persons with chronic diseases, in pregnancy or lactation women, and for children under 12 years.**

- Acer, (Arce, en español)

"Hacer saccharum", tree originating to Asia and abundant North America where 160 species, are also cultivated as ornamental trees, for the exploitation of its wood in the construction and for the elaboration of maple syrup (also called Maple honey), the largest production place of this syrup is Quebec (Canada). The leaf is the symbol of Canada, appearing on its flag. **Contraindicated for diabetics** (due to its high concentration of sugars) **and persons intolerant to glucose.**

- Acorn, (Bellota, en español)

Fruit of the oak tree "Quercus rotundifolia", is consumed raw or toasted on the grill. Within the genus'Quercus', there are numerous tree species that give acorns as the Common oak, Cork oak and the Valencian oak (all edible). **Consume in moderation, due to its high tannin content (it can become toxic).**

- Agar Agar, (Agar Agar, en español)

"Gelidium cartilagineum" or "Gelidium capense", is a powder obtained from the algae of the genera Gelidium, Euchema y Gracilaria. With it a vegetable gelatin is made that can be consumed directly or used as a food thickener. **It causes dehydration if you drink alcohol simultaneously. It can be cause of:** flatulences, meteorism, interfere with the absorption of nutritional and vitamin medications. **Contraindicated in cases of hyperthyroidism.**

- Agrimony, (Agrimonia, en español)

"Agrimonia eupatoria", originating from Europe and North Africa. It is usually used in infusion. **Occasionally it can cause constipation. It could produce a worsening in cases of peptic ulcer or gastritis. Contraindicated in pregnancy or lactation women.**

- **Ajuga iva,** (Ajuga iva, en español)

"Ajuga iva", originating from southern Europe in the Mediterranean area. The ingested infusion is made by boiling about 15 gr. for each liter of water for 15 minutes, rest and strain, take a cup on an empty stomach. **To reinforce its effects** you can have another cup in the afternoon. **Contraindicated in persons suffering from gastritis or gastroduodenal ulcer.**

- **Almond,** (Almendra, en español)

"Prunus dulcis", originating from eastern Europe and south Asia, its fruit, the almond, is used in the kitchen or as a dry fruit, **in excess it can cause small cases of diarrhoea.** The active ingredient in almonds is hydrocyanic acid, **one of the fastest and most energetic poisons known,** is formed by contact with water. An essential oil is extracted from the almond. The fruit and oil are used in medicinal treatments. **There are no known contraindications,** it is **recommended to consult** with the doctor or specialist.

- **Aloe vera,** (Aloe vera, en español)

"Aloe arborescens", is one of the pharmaceutical applications, oldest registered, is found in a Sumerian clay tablet, there are drawings of the plant on the walls of Egyptian temples. Originating from North Africa, of fleshy leaves used for the treatment of many health problems, it is recommended especially for skin problems in poultice or directly its inner gel. Two compounds, gel and juice are obtained from the leaves. **Special care with your gel, if ingested.** There are juice preparations. **Contraindicated the juices in pregnant women (abortive), or lactation, under 12 years, patients with irritable bowel, colitis, Crohn's disease, hemorrhoids, diabetics.**

- **Amaranth,** (Amaranto, en español)

"Amaranthus", American plant from north to south. It has a flower that never fades, is cultivated and used for   **...Continue on next page**

... approximately 5,000 years. **It does not have gluten**, so it is a food suitable for coeliacs. **Contraindicated by its high content of oxalic acid, in renal patients, with gout or rheumatoid arthritis.**

- Anacahuita, (Anacahuita, en español)

"Cordia boissieri", also know as Wild olive, plant of origin Chilean, does not need irrigation and capable of resisting frosts or droughts. Highly recommended to cure respiratory affections. **There are no known contraindications,** it is **recommended to consult** with the doctor or specialist.

- Annato tree, (Achiote, en español)

"Bixa Orellana", also know as Achiote tree, plant of the intertropical regions of America. Cultivated specifically in the center of Mexico since preColumbian epoch. Used as an infusion. Its fruit is used as a coloring and seasoning in popular food. **Contraindicated in pregnancy or lactation women.**

- Antennaria, Mountain everlasting, in english)

 "Antennaria dioica", plant spread throughout Europe with the exception of Portugal, Iceland, Greece and Turkey, the whole plant and herb of pink flowers (female) is used. It serves to disinfect if was in contact with sick persons or in areas with bacteria as a disinfectant for external use, macerating 1 liter of alcohol of 60º, with 40 gr. of flowers, for 20 days. Strain and use as many times as necessary, spreading in the area to absorb. **There are no known contraindications,** it is **recommended to consult** with the doctor or specialist.

- Apple, (Manzana, en español)

"Malus domestica", plant domesticated more than 15 thousand years ago, of Caucasian origin on the banks of the Caspian Sea, introduced in Europe by the Romans. It is one of the most complete and nutritious fruits. Studies are being conducted on seeds as anticarcinogenic, with surprising results and beneficial against all types of cancers.   **...Continue**

... The contraindications of apples are mainly due to their bad consumption: when they are very green, without chewing well, badly washed. **Acid apples are harmful for:** persons suffering from constipation, urethral stricture and severe stomach conditions by excess ingestion (worse if they are not mature enough). **Sour apples are contraindicated for persons with a stomach ulcer.**

- Asafoetida, (Asafétida, en español)

"Ferula assafoetida", also know a Devil's dung, it grows mainly in Afghanistan and Northern Iran, its resin is exported to India, there called Hing. It is marketed mainly in yellowish powder consisting of the mixture of ground resin with rice or wheat. **Very difficult to find, only in Indian shops.** Plant with nauseating odor in raw, cooked softens and produces a flavor similar to onion and garlic, it is used as a condiment in the form of a spice. **There are no known contraindications,** it is **recommended to consult** with the doctor or specialist.

- Ash, (Fresno, en español)

"Fraxinus excelsior", also know as European ash, originating in Europe, from Spain to Russia. Tree very popular and the most used in the public woodland. The crust, fruit and leaves contain active ingredients for medicinal purposes. The treatments are a little slower since their effects are mild and moderate, but very effective in the medium term by infusion, decoction, poultice, powder and tincture. **There are preparations** made with ash. **Consume under medical control patients with hypertension or heart disease.**

- Azuki red beans, (Azúkis, en español)

"Vigna angularis, var. nipponensis", originating from China, from there he went to Japan where it has become one of its main crops. It is consumed equal to any legume, soaking it 8 hours before cooking. Gluten-free, ideal food for any diet. With a not very high amount of fat, **it is advisable consume in moderate amounts in persons with a diet of weight loss, high uric acid, hyperthyroidism, gout and prone to flatulence.**

Descriptions of plants letter B

- Baccharises
- Banana
- Baobab tree
- Barbary fig, see Pryckli pear
- Barley
- Bay laurel
- Beans
- Bearberry, see Kinnikinnick
- Bear's breeches, see Acanthus
- Beet
- Bergamot orange
- Bigheaded thyme
- Birch
- Bistort
- Bitter lettuce
- Bitter wood
- Black mulberry / Blackberry
- Black mustard
- Black pepper
- Black samson echinacea, see Echinacea
- Black sesame
- Bloodroot
- Blue agave
- Branched horsetail, see Horsetail
- Breckland thyme
- Broad-leaved paperbark, see Niaouli
- Broadleaf cattail
- Broadleaf plantain
- Bruisewort, see Common Daisy
- Brussels sprout
- Butterfly orchid drink, see Salep drink

- Baccharises, (Carqueja, en español)

"Baccharis articulata", shrub that grows in Brazil, Argentina, Uruguay, Paraguay, Chile and spread throughout the world in rather rainy climates, or in cool places on roadsides and sites of fertile soil with moisture; **very useful to treat leprosy.** The non-woody aerial part is used. **Contraindicated in pregnancy or lactation women and diabetics.**

- Banana, (Plátano, en español)

"Musa paradisiaca", originating from India, highly nutritious and of the most caloric fruits that exist after the avocado, 100 gr. of banana contribute approximately 90 calories. Very rich in carbohydrates being one of the best ways to nourish our body with vegetable energy, very indicated in the diets of children for their properties and benefits. **In excess** can be indigestible. Diabetics should consume sparingly. **Persons with kidney or liver diseases,** it is **recommended to consult** with the doctor or specialist.

- Baobab tree, (Baobab, en español)

"Adansonia digitata", African tree, which can live up to 3,000 years, the natives call it the tree of life. Very appreciated in Europe and USA for the properties **medicinal of the superfruit** (brown or green), leaves and crust. **It has three times more vitamin C than orange,** twice as much calcium as a glass of milk and a delicious taste between pineapple and melon, excellent food to improve health and well-being helping to reduce glycemic responses. **Very difficult to get fresh,** there are prepared in the form of grajeas and essential oil, being very beneficial for many ailments. **There are no known contraindications,** it is **recommended to consult** with the doctor or specialist.

- Barley, (Cebada, en español)

"Hordeum vulgare", originating from the Middle East, food-medicine that can be consumed in diverses forms, such as semolina, cooked in any stew, salad, milk or as day water. **Contraindicated in persons with hypersensitivity to barley flour, allergic to beer, celiac and hypertensive (with assiduity).**

- Bay laurel, (Laurel, en español)

"Laurus nobilis", originating from Asia Minor and the Mediterranean basin, it can be used as ointments made from the oil of its leaves after crushing and boiling until the water is consumed. Apply by friction for relief, always diluted and in small amounts. **In topical use it can cause:** irritation and spots on the skin. You can also make essences, **...Continue on next page**

... tonics and infusions. **Contraindicated in pregnancy or lactation women, nor use their ingested oil to be abortive.**

- **Beans,** (Judías o Alubias, en español)
"Phaseolus vulgaris", originating from Central and South America, very useful food, in spite of its scarcity in calories, rich in a substance that corrects metabolic alterations. The main application of the bean is the food and fundamental element in the base of the popular cuisine of different regions, **can also be used in topical use.** When it is in development (green bean) it provides few calories, only 50 per 100 gr. The dry can even replace the meat in the feeding because in 100 gr. contains from 330 to 350 calories, plus a significant amount of vegetable proteins. **Contraindicated the dry in persons with diet of thinning, delicate stomach or intestines.**

- **Beet,** (Remolacha, en español)
"Beta vulgaris", originating from Mediterranean, very humble vegetable, but with surprising properties. **Consume with moderation persons with:** stomach acidity, gastritis, hypotension, gout, arthritis or kidney problems. **Contraindicated in pregnancy women and diabetics.**

- **Bergamot orange,** (Bergamota, en español)
 "Citrus bergamia", originally from Persia as a result of the graft between the Key lime and the Bitter Orange. The fruit and the infusions its used to healing remedies The best medicinal or cosmetic properties are achieved through its essential oil, like balm, **after its application, do not expose yourself to the sun. Do not consume the juice or fruit in combination with drugs.**

- **Bigheaded thyme,** (Tomillo cabezudo, en español)
"Coridothymus capitatus" or "Thymus capitatus", also know as Conehead thyme, or Spanish oregano, it grows throughout the southern Mediterranean basin. It is used in more or less the same way as Thyme but not as well studied. In the Balearic Islands it is the most common species. Of this variety for the curative remedies flowers are ...**Continue**

... used in infusion at the rate of one bunch per liter of water. There is honey from this Thyme. **There are no known contraindications,** it is **recommended to consult** with the doctor or specialist.

- **Birch,** (Abedul, en español)

"Betula pendula", also know as Silver birch, of origin Eurasian, almost silvery white crust. **It is used almost entirely:** leaves, flowers, sap, buds and crust of young branches. **There is essential oil, not ingest (toxic and deadly). Only for topical use and always diluted as directed by the specialist.** It is used for the infusion of tree buds and the crust. **Contraindicated during pregnancy or lactation, persons with hydrops of cardiac or renal origin, allergic and hypertensive,** (only under prescription and medical control).

- **Bistort,** (Bistorta en español)

"Polygonum bistorta", also know as European bistort, originating in the northern hemisphere and temperate zones. It is rich in nutrients such as vitamin C and carbohydrates used as a general tonic. **Its tannins can produce**: gastritis, gastroduodenal ulcus (irritate the gastric mucosa). **Do not prescribe tinctures with alcohol content to minors or people in the process of becoming alcohol-free.**

- **Bitter lettuce,** (Lechuga virosa, en español)

"Lactuca virosa L", originating from Central Asia, Egyptian papyri date their use for various ailments towards 1,600 BC of yellow flowers and unpleasant smell. **It is used in substitution of opium, but without harmful side effects.** At present it is mainly used as a calming, in syrup and associated with Hops. **Do not exceed the indicated doses, use only under medical supervision.** You can use the common lettuce already spiked. **The juice or latex is toxic.**

- **Bitter wood,** (Quassia, en español)

"Quassia Amara" or "Picrama excelsa", originating from Tropical America and one of the most bitter plants that exist. Very used for cosmetic and medicinal purposes. Stands out for being a **...Continue on next page**

... natural insecticide very efficient to not contain toxic substances, does not affect pets or children and repels all kinds of insects being economic and ecological. **The crust in infusion only under specialist control. Quassia vinegar is also used. Contraindicated during the menstrual period (may cause colics, pain and increased uterine tone) and pregnant women (abortive).**

- Black mulberry / Blackberry, (Morera negra / Mora negra, en español)

"Morus nigra", originating from Southwest Asia, the properties of this tree reside in the leaves, root and crust. Its fruits because they contain a lot of sugar, salt, acids, pectin and gum. With the white berries or white mulberries of the "Morus alba" a good syrup is made for colds in the respiratory tract. **There are no known contraindications,** it is **recommended to consult** with the doctor or specialist.

- Black mustard, (Mostaza negra, en español)

"Brassica nigra", is similar to the Collard greens. Hairy at the base and without hair on the rest of the stem, straight and with extended branches. Originating from Mediterranea basin, it grows cultivated or feral between the harvests and wastelands, of flavor stronger than the white one. There are preparations for different purposes, **even a sweet mustard made** for the little ones. You can consume the seed directly, sprinkling the meals and in infusions. **In topical use it can** generate inflammations in the skin. **Contraindicated in persons with inflammation and intestinal, urinary and stomach discomfort.**

- Black pepper, (Pimienta negra, en español)

"Piper nigrum", originating from India, one of the most famous spices and used to seasoning. It comes from the same tree as the black or pink one, it is collected with the immature grain, when it dries it turns black and its skin wrinkles. Its flavor is very characteristic and somewhat spicy, due to the **piperine** content, its spicy power would be 1% of the capsaicin in the Chile peper. In infusions, better mask by its strong flavor, there are bags made with Pepper. **Consume with moderation persons ...Continue**

... who suffer: gastric ulcer, stomach acidity or gastritis. **In excess** it can cause seizures. **Caution, if it reaches the lungs raw in children under 6 years, can cause death, it is advised to use powder.**

- Black sesame, (Sésamo, en español)

"Sesamum indicum", originating from India and Africa, from where it arrived in America transported by the slaves. It can be consumed directly in salads, sweets, rice, grilled or sautéed vegetables. **Use only under medical prescription:** persons with liver or kidney disease. **Contraindicated the esential oil in pregnancy women.**

- Bloodroot, (Sanguinaria del Canadá, en español)

"Sanguinaria canadensis", originating from USA and Canada, of white or pink flowers. **For curative purposes, the leaves are used in infusion. There are dental products with bloodroot. Before using to consult** with the doctor or specialist, It has toxic alkaloids like Opium and can irritate the mucous membrane. **Contraindicated in pregnancy or lactation women.**

- Blue agave, (Agave tequilana, en español)

"Agave tequilana", also know as Tequila agave, originating from Mesoamerica, with it Tequila is made, but it is mainly used for its medicinal properties for both topical and internal use by infusions of the leaves, if you want to sweeten, see the sweeteners. With this plant is also used made a syrup that serves as a sweetener. If there are **allergic reactions** such as **difficulty breathing, rash, swelling of the lips or tongue, seek urgent medical attention. It can produce:** diarrhea and upset stomach. **Contraindicated during pregnancy or lactation women.**

- Breckland thyme, (Serpol, en español)

"Thymus serpyllum", originating from center of Europe, in valleys and mountains up to 2,500 m., stony and clear steep areas of the forests. Plant related to the Thyme with whom it shares numerous medicinal properties known and exploited about 2,000 years BC. For curative purposes herbs and flowers are used **in controlled doses,** as **...Continue on next page**

... an infusion made by pouring in a ¼ liter of water 2 tablespoons of coffee, with herbs and flowers of Breckland thyme, to rest for 10 minutes, strain and drink 2 or 3 cups a day. They exist in tinctures and oils, you can also season the salads. **There are no known contraindications,** it is **recommended to consult** with the doctor or specialist.

- Broadleaf cattail, (Tifa, en español)

"Typha latifolia", very widespread plant in aquatic areas, river edges and freshwater lakes throughout the northern subtropical hemisphere, usually forming large groupings of round stems up to 3 meters high, with leaves of 150 cm. of length. For curative remedies its roots are used and to a lesser extent the seeds. In topical use between 50 and 100 gr. of root per liter of wáter. **There are no known contraindications,** it is **recommended to consult** with the doctor or specialist.

- Broadleaf plantain, (Llantén mayor, en español) "Plantago major",

originating from Europe, North and Central America, plant large and green leaves, the leaf is used in infusion, or its juice to treat diseases. The seed can be sprinkled on foods or salads. The root is a powerful remedy against the venom of the rattlesnake. **Contraindicated in pregnant women (abortive), persons allergic to melon or hyperthyroidism.**

- Brussels sprout, (Col de Bruselas, en español)

"Brassica oleracea var. Gemmifera", its origin is from the surroundings of Brussels, it has been known since the 16th century, there are references that started to be fully in the 19th century. It can be used both internally and in topical use. When they boil they lose much of their qualities therefore it is recommended to take them steamed or raw. **Consume with moderation persons with a tendency to bad digestion or meteorism.**

Descriptions of plants letter C

- Cacao or Cocoa
- Calamus
- California, see Yellow pepper
- Camomile, see Chamomile
- Cantaloupe
- Cardamom
- Carob tree
- Castor oil
- Catnip
- Cecropia
- Chachacoma
- Chalk milkwort
- Chamomile
- Chard
- Cherimoya
- Cherry
- Cherrys tree
- Chestnut fruit
- Chestnut tree
- Chickpea
- Chicory
- Chilean myrtle
- Chives
- Cinnamon / Cinnamon tree
- Cinnamon with honey
- Cissampelos pareira
- Clary sage or Clary
- Clementina
- Coconut tree/Coconut
- Common Daisy
- Common fleabane
- Common gypsyweed, see Heath speedwell
- Common milkwort
- Common primrose, see English primrose
- Conehead thyme, see Bigheaded thyme
- Conker tree, see Horse-chesnut
- Coriander
- Cornflower
- Cornstartch
- Cowslip primrose
- Cranesbills, see Geranium
- Cream of tartar
- Curry

- **Cacao,** (Cacao, en español)

"Theobroma cacao", also know as Cocoa, of Mexican origin, in pre-Hispanic Mexico (Mayan culture) it was used as a currency of exchange. **Powerful food with incredible properties and benefits, for ...Continue on next page**

... our physical and mental health, emotions. It stimulates, comforts and revives our organism. One of the best known foods that exist, especially because you get one of the most consumed desserts par excellence: the **chocolate. Contraindicated its consumption in persons with constipation, hemorrhoids, hypertensive or nervous states (to contain traces of caffeine).**

- Calamus, (Cálamo aromático, en español)
"Acorus calamus", also know as Sweet flag, it grows in the northern hemisphere on the banks of rivers and marshes. The medicinal use is very diverse for a long time, It gives off a pleasant smell, for the medicinal remedies the rhizome and the stems are used. **Discontinuous treatment is recommended,** one of its components **is suspected of producing cancer and toxic to the central nervous system. Contraindicated the essential oil in pregnancy or** lactation women **and under 2 years.**

- Cantaloupe, (Melón cantalupo o Melón francés, en español)
 "Cucumis melo cantalupensis", also know as Spanspek, it growns naturally in Asia and Africa for more than 4,000 years. France is the main producer of this variety, orange-colored pulp. There are countries that receive guests sprinkled with sugar, ginger and very cold melon. **There are no known contraindications,** it is **recommended to consult** with the doctor or specialist.

- Cardamom, (Cardamomo, en español)
"Elettaria cardamomum", originating from the southwestern of India. One of the most appreciated and expensive spices in the world. Contains essential oils, starch, fiber, beneficial as a nutritious, energizing food and to maintain intestinal regularity. Very aromatic plant to sprinkle on hot food or drinks. **Contraindicated its essential oil in topical use to children under 6 years and persons with respiratory allergies. Contraindicated ingested by pregnancy or lactation women, children under 6 years, persons with respiratory allergies, gastritis, ...Continue**

... gastroduodenal ulcers, irritable bowel syndrome, ulcerative colitis, Crohn's disease, hepatopathies, epilepsy, Parkinson's or other neurological diseases.

- Carob tree, (Algarroba, en español)

"Ceratonia siliqua", of origin European, plant of great hardiness and resistance to drought. The fruit / seed of powdered pods or flour is consumed to coat food, it is very dark. Contains carbohydrates, vitamins A, B, folic acid, C, E, minerals and fiber. Its used to biscuits, ideal for diabetics and minors to be sweet, the dough is a little dry. **May** cause **constipation. Diabetics** should **consult their doctor** to readjust the dose if necessary.

- Castor oil, (Aceite de ricino, en español)

"Ricinus communis", originating from North Africa, plant similar to the fig tree, oil quite controversial some claim that it has an important toxic potential. But it is an oil that has many properties and uses different from the more conventional and very beneficial in external use like hair, eyelashes, eyebrows or fingernails and lips, warts. **It has many contraindications ingested. Use only topically.**

- Catnip, (Gatera, en español)

"Nepeta cataria", originating from Europe, the Romans already used it for curative purposes, **also against smallpox and scarlet fever.** Its name is due to its effects on the behavior of cats, both in domestic animals and in larger ones (even in big cats). It is consumed mainly in the form of tea, preparing the infusion with a teaspoon of the plant for each cup of water, boil, let stand 3 minutes, strain and drink. It can also be used in juice, tincture, poultice, chew and even smoked. **Contraindicated in pregnant women.**

- Cecropia, (Ambay, en español)

"Cecropia adenopus", tree originating in south America in its jungle areas. Its leaves and crust are used in infusion, **in topical use without sweetening.** Used for curative purposes by the aborigines from Mexico to the northeast region of Argentina, it continues to be a remedy **...Continue on next page**

... of habitual use in the popular medicine of center and south of America. **Contraindicated in pregnancy or lactation women.**

- Chachacoma, (Chachacoma, en español)

"Senecio oreophyton", originating from argentinean-chilean mountain range and used since time immemorial by the aborigines of the area. There are several types, as a medicinal herb two have been recognized, **a white call,** whose healing properties and appearances are identical, differing only by the white color taken by the leaves and branches one of them. The usual form is the infusion, there are also syrups, and tinctures. **There are no known contraindications,** it is **recommended to consult** with the doctor or specialist.

- Chalk milkwort, (Polygala calcárea, en español)

"Polygala calcárea", is found in Great Britain, France, Switzerland, Germany, Belgium, Spain, especially in calcareous and rocky terrain. Blooms in early March and se caracteriza por sus flores de color intensamente azul. Planta de poco uso medicinal por desconocimiento, pero es un excelente mucolítico, se utiliza en infusión tomando 2 tazas al día. **There are no known contraindications,** it is **recommended to consult** with the doctor or specialist.

- Chamomile, (Manzanilla común, en español)

"Chamaemelum nobile", also know as Camomile, originating from Europe, annual aromatic herb of the family of the compounds, can reach up to 60 cm. high. It grows on cultivated land, on sandy soil and barrens. The usual use is infusion ingested or in topical use. There is also essential oil, which should **not be mixed with alcohol. Contraindicated the essential oil in pregnant women (abortive), under 6 years.**

- Chard, (Acelga, en español)

"Beta vulgaris var. Cicla", originating from Mediterranean, green leafy vegetable with very beneficial nutritional properties, its cultivation today has spread all over the world. They are consumed fresh in **...Continue**

... salads, green smoothies, rolls, etc., are taken full advantage of of their nutritional properties. **Do not consume excess persons with:** kidney stones. **Contraindicated in people with stomach problems or diarrhea.**

- Cherimoya, (Chirimoya, en español)

"Annona cherimola", originating from the Andean zone bordering Ecuador and Peru. Spain is the world's leading producer of cherimoya with 80% of the total. It does not need any treatment, it is eaten as is. **It is not recommended for dessert after a copious meal.** When consuming for the first time persons with problems of constipation may appear intestinal alteration, but it is really helping to correct your problem. Fruit of easy digestion very advisable in weak persons, convalescents, elderly, in dyspepsia and especially in children and pregnant women. Some products extracted from the seeds from cherimoya They have been applied successfully in investigations for the treatment of lice, dysentery, headaches, gout and stones. **Potassium source, persons with kidney failure should be careful. Consume with moderation diabetics.**

- Cherry, (Cereza o Guinda, en español)

Fruit of the Cherry tree, considered the super fruit, with multiple properties and health benefits. No limit in taking all the fruit you want. **There are no known contraindications,** it is **recommended to consult** with the doctor or specialist.

- Cherrys tree, (Cerezo, en español)

"Prunus cerasus", originating from Europe and Southeast Asia, are medicinal properties of fruits, leaves and even their stems. Is used as tisane a handful of stems in 1 liter of water, or the fresh juice of its fruits. **There are no known contraindications,** it is **recommended to consult** with the doctor or specialist.

- Chestnut fruit, (Castaña, en español)

It is the fruit of the chestnut tree, cooked is delicious, it is made the exquisite Marron glacé (original Asturian form, **...Continue on next page**

... but commercialized with that name by the French). We know it in the cold months, and the best way to consume is roasted. **Consume with moderation pregnant women. Contraindicated in diabetics.**

- Chestnut tree, (Castaño, en español)

"Castanea sativa", tree originating from southern Europe and Asia Minor. It is used for medicinal remedies the bark, wood, leaves and buds. **There are no known contraindications,** it is **recommended to consult** with the doctor or specialist.

- Chickpea, (Garbanzo, en español)

"Cicer arietinum", its origin is believed in the eastern Mediterranean zone, legume rich in slowabsorbing carbohydrates, so it provides energy, but with very controlled blood sugar levels. **Control its use in:** slimming diets, with high uric acid levels, hyperthyroidism, goiter or thyroid nodules. **Persons who suffer from flatulence or can not consume a lot of insoluble fiber is better to eat eliminating the skin once cooked.**

- Chicory, (Achicoria, en español)

"Cichorium intybus", of origin Europe in a wild way, with numerous medical properties. Known for being an excellent substitute for coffee. Two cups of chicory infusion per day or a single cup before dinner are recommended. **Contraindicated in persons with low blood pressure, or if they have gallstones.**

- Chilean myrtle, (Palo colorado, en español)

"Luma apiculata", known locally as Red myrtle, very twisted trunk tree, originating from Chile and Argentina, grows near the river courses. With its fruits, the indigenous people elaborate the "Chicha". **There are no known contraindications,** it is **recommended to consult** with the doctor or specialist.

- Chives, (Cebollino, en español)

"Allium schoenoprasum", originating from the extreme north of the lands that today are part of Canada and Siberia. It can be used in **...Continue**

... soups, salads, sauces, tortillas, creams and various meals. For health benefits should be consumed on a daily basis, **not in large quantities.** Very easy to cultivate and in little space, you can have at home a pot of chives for fresh daily consumption. **There are no known contraindications,** it is **recommended to consult** with the doctor or specialist.

- Cinnamon / Cinnamon tree, (Canela / Canelo, en español)

"Cinnamomum verum" or "Drimys winteri", from Patagonia in Chile and Argentina. Evergreen tree, and sacred to the Mapuche people. The cinnamon is extracted from its crust to sprinkle, the infusion is made by adding hot water in a cup with bark, rest 5 minutes and drink hot. Giving flavor is not the only function, it has a lot of medicinal properties. **Contraindicated in pregnancy or lactation women.**

- Cinnamon with honey, (Canela con miel, en español)

Cinnamon and honey are two nutritious foods, **(use honey from 1 year).** It is prepared by mixing the honey and cinnamon until it is quite thick. Store the preparation in a hermetically sealed glass jar. Keep in a cool place, it keeps well for quite some time without the need for any preservative for the properties of both. A tablespoon with warm water daily cinnamon and honey has many properties for health and also with a delicious flavor. It can be mixed with other drinks.

- Cissampelos pareira, (Pareira brava, en español)

"Cissampelos Pareira" originating from Central and South America, wild plant that grows in all the warm and temperate regions of the world. Used in traditional Chinese and Ayurveda medicine since ancient times, as well as in Mexican indigenous medicine and other places in the world. All parts of the plant have healing properties. **Dosage under medical prescription** used in powder or capsules. **The excess, due to its diuretic effect, can produce various disorders.**

- Clary sage, (Salvia romana, en español)

"Salvia sclarea", also know as Clary, originating from Mediterranean basin to central Asia. **Do not drink alcohol using the essential oil,** exaggerate the alcoholic effects, drunkenness, subsequent discomfort or cause drowsiness. **Contraindicated the essential oil in pregnancy women, by stimulating menstrual flow.**

- Clementina, (Clementina, en español)

"Citrus clementina", originating in Asia, although it is almost the same and belongs to the same variety of citrus, it is a hybrid between Tangerina and Bitter orange, it has no seeds and is sweeter in flavor. You can make an infusion with its shell to mask flavors of other infusions. **There are no known contraindications,** it is **recommended to consult** with the doctor or specialist.

- Coconut tree / Coconut, (Cocotero/coco, en español)

 "Cocos nucifera", tree of unknown origin, Asian or Caribbean, does not tolerate the cold. Its fruit, the coconut, is the largest seed that exists of benefits and health properties consumed occasionally and naturally, unpackaged. Coconut oil contains high levels of lauric acid, and can be used for cooking. **Contraindicated in persons with some cardiovascular disease (contains many saturated fatty acids), high cholesterol or with weight control diet.**

- Common Daisy, (Margarita, en español)

"Bellis perennis", also know as Daisy or Bruisewort, originating from western, central and northern Europe. Its flowers and leaves are used for the treatment of a wide variety of disorders. **The ingested infusions (consult with the doctor or specialist),** it can affect and **cause blood clots.** It can also **stunt growth (not scientifically proven).** Better to use in topical use, **especially and always, in under 12 years.**

- Common fleabane, (Pulicaria, en español)

"Pulicaria dysenterica", also know as Meadow false fleabane, widely used since antiquity, it grows in coastal areas or near water and wild in southern Europe and North Africa. It is collected in the middle of summer, when the active principles are more intense. It is used in ingested infusion or in topical use at a rate of 30 gr. per liter of water. **There are no known contraindications,** it is **recommended to consult** with the doctor or specialist.

- Common milkwort, (Polígala común, en español)

"Polygala vulgaris", originating from Europe and Mediterrnean basin, it grows in pine forests and meadows of few nutrients. The rhizome and the root are used, sometimes the whole plant in infusion, which is prepared with 12 gr. per 1/4 liter of water. Exists in tincture, syrup, fluid and dry extracts. **There are no known contraindications,** it is **recommended to consult** with the doctor or specialist.

- Coriander, (Cilantro, en español)

"Coriandrum sativum", originating from southern Europe and northern Africa, plant similar to parsley and with multiple health properties, remains have been found of this herb in the tombs of the Egyptian pharaohs. Good source of vitamin K., is used sprinkled or minced in soups and salads, you can also make infusions. **Contraindicated during in pregnant women (abortive), or lactation.**

- Cornflower, (Aciano, en español)

"Centaurea cyanus", originating from Mediterranean, among the most outstanding medicinal plants in the natural kit is undoubtedly the Cornflower. **The persons with medication permanently, before using, consult with your doctor or specialist.**

- Cornstarch, (Maizena o Maicena, en español)

The correct definition is corn starch flour. **A special section is made in this case, to highlight the properties of this starch in very specific ailments**. The description and properties of this, obviously, is that of the corn plant.

- Cowslip primrose, (Hierba de san Pedro, en español)

"Primula officinalis" or "Primula veris", originating from Europe and Asia, it is edible and for seasoning. It has a stem with a lot of villi in all its extension of aroma quite unpleasant that spreads instantly. The infusion has a pleasant flavor. Very good balm, can be administered even in childhood. **There are no known contraindications,** it is **recommended to consult** with the doctor or specialist.

- Cream of tartar, (Crémor tártaro, en español)

"Potassium bitartrate", it is an acid by-product of wine, when the grape juice ferments to become wine, the sediment remaining in the barrels is purified and converted into white powder It is advisable to consume 2,000 mg. per day in persons over 18 years. **Do not consume more than 1 teaspoon of dessert persons with kidney disease, congestive heart failure, with medications that decrease the ability to excrete potassium in the kidneys.**

- Curry, (Curry en español)

"Murraya koenigii", the tree is originating from India, here it is **the curry powder** as a mixture of herbs, a condiment quite popular in India. Depending on the type of herbs that are mixed **in the preparation**, there are three variations: **Green Curry, Red Curry and Yellow Curry.** Its therapeutic powers, due to the large amounts of curcumin contained, allow us to compare it with the spice Turmeric. **Contraindicated in pregnancy or lactation women, in cases kidney stones, gastritis and gastric ulcers.**

Descriptions of plants letter D

- Daisy, see Common Daisy
- Devil's dung, see Asafoetida
- Devil's backbone plant, see Kalanchoe
- Durmast oak
- Dyer's greenweed or Dyer's broom

- Dyer's greenweed, (Retama de los tintoreros, en español)

"Genista tinctoria", also know as Dyer's broom, it grows in pasture areas in North America and Europe, from the 15th century studies, previously used only to dye fabrics permanently. Therapeutically it is used in infusion made with 5 gr. of freshly opened flowers added to a liter of water. Boil for ten minutes, strain and drink 3 cups throughout the day, avoid overdose (contains alkaloids). **Do not collect, it is easy to confuse with another broom (green dye) for its flowers,** better to buy in specialized shops. **Contraindicated in persons with hypertension.**

- Durmast oak, (Roble albar, en español)

"Querus petraea", originating from North Hemisphere, species that groups different species. The crust of the branches is used, although the leaves and the fruit are also used. The 3 mm thick spring crust is used. **Contraindicated in pregnancy or lactation women and persons with medication that causes hepatotoxic damage.**

Descriptions of plants letter E

- East Asian arrowoot, see Kudzu
- Eastern black walnut
- Echinacea
- Eggshell and Egg white
- Elder or Elderberry
- Elms
- English primrose
- Erythraea chilensis
- Escarole

- Eucalyptus
- European ash, see Ash
- European bistort, see Bistort
- European bugleweed, see Virginia water horehound
- European searocket
- Evening primrose

- Eastern black walnut, (Nogal americano, en español)

"Juglans nigra", originating from North America, used in indigenous medicine for centuries, introduced in Europe in 1629 to soften the skin. Its crust has powerful astringent properties. Its leaves are used in infusion. There are capsules (**it is advisable to follow indications,** recommend two 500 mg capsules three times a day, preferably with meals). **Contraindicated in pregnancy or lactation women, patients with liver, kidney, gastrointestinal, medicated for blood pressure, or with cough accompanied by fever.**

- Echinacea, (Equinácea, en español)

"Echinacea angustifolia", also know as Narrowleaved purple coneflower or Black samson echinacea, originating from North American prairies. Without a doubt, it is **the most wellknown and studied plant** of medicinal herbs to stimulate or enhance the immune system and increase the body's defenses by activating the production of leukocytes (in the lungs, colds, rheumatism, coughs). Unlike a vaccine that is activated only against a specific disease, the "echinacea" **fight against all types of infections,** by stimulating the general activity of the responsible cells. **Some persons experience allergic reactions such as: skin rashes, nausea, stomach problems.** There are capsules (even for children over 6 years old), dry and fluid extract, creams and tincture for topical use in lotions and dressings. For infusions, use the leaves and the dry extract of the root and, depending on how concentrated the dose is, you can drink up to five cups of tea on the first day and then reduce the number of cups **...Continue**

... as symptoms subside. **Very cautions the asthmatics. Do not prolong your intake for more than two / three weeks. Avoid when taking immunosuppressants.**

- Eggshell and Egg white, (Cáscara y Clara de huevo, en español)

Exception of the book, added by being habitual in all households and a good resource. Its high concentration of calcium and the adjacent layer is ideal for home remedies, here we will treat some of the most common.

- Elder, (Saúco, en español)

"Sambucus nigra", also know as Elderberry, originating from Europe and northwest of Africa. The infusion of flowers or tincture, are used for the upper respiratory tract, being anti-inflammatory and expectorant. **Contraindicated in pregnancy women, or in patients who get worse if they lose a lot of fluid.**

- Elms, (Olmo, en español)

"Ulmus minor" or "Ulmus carpinfolia", originating from Northern hemisphere of Eurasia and America. **It can cause:** hypersensitivity and contact allergy. **There are no known contraindications,** it is **recommended to consult** with the doctor or specialist.

- English primrose, (Oreja de oso, en español)

"Primula vulgaris", also know as Common primrose, originating from Europe, but also in the Far East and Siberia. Often gathering in Belarus, regions of St. Petersburg (Leningrad) and Kaliningrad). The infusion of its flowers and leaves in moderate doses is used. **The excess causes:** vomiting, diarrhea, nausea and other side effects. **Contraindicated in persons with acute kidney diseases.**

- Erythraea chilensis, (Canchalagua, en español)

"Centaurium canchalahuen", canchalahuen it means **"flank pain".** Andean plant with pink and very bitter flowers, of the **...Continue on next page**

... most appreciated in their medicine. **Do not use in prolonged use. There are no known contraindications,** it is **recommended to consult** with the doctor or specialist.

- Escarole, (Escarola, en español)

"Cichorium inthybus var. Foliossum", its origin of wild chicory is believed. Also known as bitter chicory, both as plants developed from the commercialized endive (white-leaf escarole). Ancient civilizations soon discovered that this vegetable was keeping in its curly and tasty leaves a good number of properties for its high content of vitamin C, which favor the formation of collagen and red blood cells, increasing the absorption of iron and folic acid. The usual way to consume is in salads. **There are no known contraindications,** it is **recommended to consult** with the doctor or specialist.

- Eucalyptus, (Eucalyptus o Eucalipto, en español)

"Eucalyptus", originating from Australia and Tasmania, it arrived in Europe at the end of the 19th century of cleaning up the swampy regions. It is used, above all, the leaves of the species "globulus" by means of decoction vapors or in infusions. **Caution with your essential oil** can reduce the effect of other medications. **Use under medical supervision in any form in: pregnancy or lactation women,** it can stimulate the liver enzymes of the fetus and the baby. **Contraindicated in case of gastrointestinal inflammations, bile ducts or hepatic insufficiency.**

- European searocket, (Oruga marítima, en español)

"Cakile marítima", originating from the coasts bathed by the Atlantic in the northern hemisphere, Mediterranean basin and Black Sea. Very grass and florida almost the whole year, they lie down easily, with a long, branched and hardened root. For medicinal purposes, fresh stems and branches are of interest. It is used mainly against scurvy, by the large amount of vitamin C. Plant with little medical application today to be **...Continue**

... replaced by others of the same characteristics and more complete. It uses the juice that is extracted from the freshly picked green leaves and strain to drink. **There are no known contraindications,** it is **recommended to consult** with the doctor or specialist.

- Evening primrose, (Onagra en español)

"Oenothera", also know as Sundrops, originating from North America, the native Indians used it for nutritional and medicinal purposes. In the 18th century, Europeans considered it a miracle herb. It produces different leaves during the first and second year and its fruit is in the form of a capsule. The evening primrose oil is obtained after the cold pressure of the fruit. **3 pills** are consumed throughout the day **(follow the specialist's instructions).** For topical use the oil is used. The flowers of evening primrose are can be used to flavor certain salads. **The side effects could be:** headache, nausea and diarrhea. **Do not use for epileptics.**

Descriptions of plants letter F

- **Fennel**
- **Fenugreek**
- **Fiddle dock**
- **Fig tree / Fig**

- Fennel, (Hinojo, en español)

"Foeniculum vulgare", only one species of its kind, originating from Mediterranean coast where it grows in the wild. It is used as an infusion. **Contraindicated in patients with breast cancer or persons with hyperthyroidism. The essential oil its contraindicated in pregnancy or lactation women and under 6 years.**

- Fenugreek, (Alholva, en español)

"Trigonella foenum-graecum", originating in Southwest Asia. **Its benefits cover the entire range of pathologies from external to internal applications,** is in full study by science, since it seems to have many applications on health. **More than 100 gr. per ...Continue on next page**

... day can cause: diarrhea and nausea. **May interact with:** hypoglycemic medications and cause a decrease in blood sugar levels very below of safe levels for diabetic patients. **Contraindicated in pregnant women (it can cause a drop in your blood sugar levels, tremors, feeling hungry and excessive sweating).**

- Fiddle dock, (Romanza, en español)

"Rumex pulcher", originating from Mediterranean basin, invasive plant similar to the Bitter dock, it differs in its leaf, this one is **of heart-shaped base.** With flowers in the armpits of the upper leaves. Exclusive use as a vegetable and cooked like Spinach. **Contraindicated in arthritic, rheumatic, with gout or kidney disease.**

- Fig tree / Fig, (Higuera / Higo, en español)

"Ficus carica", originating from Southwest Asia, since antiquity it was attributed to the fig tree medicinal virtues both in leaves and in its fruit. **Latex is toxic to the skin.** One of the most common forms is infusion. The fig **is not suitable for diabetics, a high consumption can cause diarrhea.**

Descriptions of plants letter G

- Garden angelica
- Garden nasturtium
- Garden sage, see Sage
- Garden yellow loosestrife, see Loosestrife
- Garlic
- Geranium
- Grapefruit
- Grape of the bear, see Kinnikinnick
- Grapevine / Grape
- Great mullein, see Mullein
- Ginger
- Gladiolus
- Green pepper
- Grenadia
- Gum arabic tree
- Gypsywort, see Virginia wáter horehound

- Garden angelica, (Angelica, en español)

"Angelica archangelica", originating from northern Europe and Syria. Its leaves are used to flavor fruit compotes, jams, broths and liqueurs. Fresh leaves and stems are used in soups and salads. **Avoid sun exposure in your treatment. Contraindicated your essential oil internally during the pregnancy or lactation women, under 6 years, patients with epilepsy, Parkinson's or other neurological diseases. It is not recommended in any way in pregnancy or lactation women and diabetics.**

- Garden nasturtium, (Mastuerzo, en español)

"Tropaeolum majus", originating from South America, perennial plant, crawling and climbing plant very striking for its flowers, is used to decorate gardens and outdoor spaces. In Europe it has acclimated in coastal areas as a wild plant. The whole plant is used, it has fleshy and branched stems, green leaves and yellow or red flowers. **Contraindicated in persons with hypothyroidism.**

- Garlic, (Ajo, en español)

"Allium sativum", probably of Asian origin, it has been cultivated for more than 7,000 years. Food of high nutritional value. Significantly reduces the toxicity of lead and associated symptoms. Consumed packaging to the brine does not cause halitosis and its intake is not annoying. **It can cause:** heartburn, flatulence or gas, belching, vomiting or diarrhea. **Avoid with food or anticoagulant supplements such as:** the Evening primrose oil, Grapefruit or Black willow. **Avoid also before or after surgery,** by decreasing the healing of wounds. **Excess consumption can cause problems:** in diabetics, bleeding or excessive anticoagulation. **Caution may interact with medications:** as anticoagulants, drugs for the heart, hypertension, contraceptives, corticosteroids, for cholesterol. **It is recommended not to take more than 2 cloves** of raw garlic on an empty stomach a day for persons with high or low blood pressure. **Contraindicated in pregnancy or lactation women, under 3 years, during menstruation, persons with hyperthyroidism.**

- Geranium, (Geranio, en español)

"Pelargonium × hortorum", also know as Cranesbills, it's a hybrid with the Mallow, also know as Geranium, originating from Mediterranean basin, grows in all the temperate zones of the world with more than 400 species. Beautiful plant with very nice smell that it also serves to keep away mosquitoes pests in the garden. There are references to ancient Egypt in its use as a holistic treatment over time to improve physical, mental and emotional health. The different parts of the plant can be used in the form of oil: leaves, stems, roots, flowers. **Do not use the oil ingested in children under 6 years.**

- Ginger, (Jengibre, en español)

"Zingiber officinale", originating from Asia and East for the USA, tuber of spicy flavor covered with brown skin. It is a sensational plant also as an ingredient widely used in gastronomy. Traditionally, ginger has been and it is one of the most popular plants in traditional Chinese medicine. It can be used sprinkled, as an ingredient in stews or in infusion (masking, can be unpleasant). **Contraindicated in pregnancy or lactation women, diabetics, persons with gallstones, gastritis, gastroduodenal ulcers, irritable colon, colitis, Crohn's disease, in treatment with medicines for blood circulation, anticoagulants, or against the hypertension.**

- Gladiolus, (Gladiolo, en español)

"Gladiolus", also know as Plural gladioli, originating from Mediterranean basin, Asia and tropical Africa, with more than 200 species. Beautiful plant, very common in burials, the rhizome is used. The usual is the infusion that is made when boiling 350 gr. of wáter with 5gr. of Gladiolus, 5gr. of Licorice y 5gr. of Elecampane. Allow to stand for approximately 20 minutes. Filter and sweeten with honey (over 1 year) or to taste, see sweeteners. **There are no known contraindications,** it is **recommended to consult** with the doctor or specialist.

- Grapefruit, (Pomelo, en español)

"Citrus × paradisi", originating from Southeast Asian, Its cultivation has been spreading to countries with a similar climate. It's like a larger orange and yellow as lemon, There are varieties of green and pinkish colors, with a slightly bitter taste but very pleasant to the palate. It is recommended to consume the whole fruit preferably as juice. It is **recommended to consult** with the doctor or specialist **before consuming,** you can interact with medications **from persons with:** kidney problems, hypertension and heart conditions **(Ciclosporin, Felodipine, Nifedipine, Verapamil).**

- Grapevine / Grape, (Vid / Uva, en español)

"Vitis vinífera", the origin of grapes grown in Europe is believed to be in the Caspian Sea region. For curative remedies the leaves, fruits and oil extracted from the seeds are used. In topical use what is known as "water or sap of vine shoots or red vine" is very appropriate. It is the sap of the plant that is obtained in spring, usually in the month of March before the leaves come out. A tender branch is cut and a liquid is allowed to distill through the cut and collect in a very clean glass. **Do not use** dosage **forms with alcohol content in under 6 years or persons with ethyl** problems. **There are no known contraindications,** it is **recommended to consult** with the doctor or specialist.

- Green pepper, (Pimiento verde, en español)

"Capsicum annuum", originating from America, being known in Europe by the Spanish in the 16th century, it is the most immature of peppers, bitter taste with half of vitamin C and a tenth of vitamin A compared to red or yellow color. Powerful antioxidant, vitamin C is necessary for proper absorption of iron if deficient. The green pepper is among the lowest calorie foods, 100 gr. contains only 19.68 kcal. **There are no known contraindications,** it is **recommended to consult** with the doctor or specialist.

- Grenadia, (Granadilla, en español)

"Passiflora ligularis", also know as Sweet granadilla, climbing plant of the Andes, domesticated in the pre-Inca era. Type of passion fruit whose pulp is full of hard blackish seeds, surrounded by a light gray transparent gelatinous ring and aromatic acid flavor, it is recommended to **integrate the baby** as one of the first foods. **As side effects we can cite:** nausea, vomiting, abdominal pain and diarrhea, due to excessive consumption. **Contraindicated to allergy sufferers, in persons diabetics** (due to its high content of sugars), **in hepatics or with a diet** (due to its caloric intake).

- Gum arabic tree, (Acacia, en español)

"Acacia nilotica", species of acacia native to Africa and the Indian subcontinent. The most common form of use is infusion ingested or in topical use. **The allergics should consult a doctor.** The parts that are used are flowers and leaves. **Contraindicated in pregnant and lactating women.**

Descriptions of plants letter H

- Hamamelis virginiana
- Hawkweed
- Hazel
- Hazelnut
- Heath speedwell
- Helychrysum
- Henna tree
- Herb Bennet
- Hibiscus, see Roselle
- High mallow, see Mallow
- Honey
- Honeysuckle
- Hops
- Horehound
- Horse-chestnut
- Horsetail

- Hamamelis virginiana, (Hamamelis, en español)

"Hamamelis virginiana", also know as Witch hazel, originating from North America, widely used in topical use since ancient times as a traditional and effective remedy by Native Americans. It is used **...Continue**

... for both internal and external use. **Use only in topical use for children under 12 years. In** internal use **the infusion or drinkable drops** (found in specialized stores) should be consumed **with caution internally, never for long periods of time. Contraindicated in pregnancy or lactation women, under 6 years, anemic, persons with ulcers or heartburn, Crohn's disease, colitis, constipation, with liver disease, or on anticoagulant treatment.**

- Hawkweed, (Vellosilla, en español)

"Hieracium pilosella", also know as Mouse-ear hawkweed, originating from Europe and Asia, it grows well in the sun and in dry climates, sandy soils, not very fertile, pastures, rocks, walls, it is quite characteristic, stands out for its striking yellow color. It can be used whole and dry in the form of infusions prepared by pouring 10 gr. in 1 liter of boiling water, leave to simmer 10 minutes more. Filter and drink two cups a day in the morning and noon. There are preparations of tinctures and capsules, possessing the advantage of not being toxic, even in case of prolonged use. **There are no known contraindications,** it is **recommended to consult** with the doctor or specialist.

- Hazel, (Avellano, en español)

"Corylus avellana", treenative to the Mediterranean. It uses the infusions of crusts and leaves ingested or in topical use (washed and in compresses), **Contraindicated in persons with gastritis and gastroduodenal ulcer (may cause discomfort and constipation).**

- Hazelnut, (Avellana, en español)

Fruit of the tree "Corylus avellana", natural source of protein and an excellent source of energy easily assimilable by our organism, rich in fat, about 70%, with proteins and carbohydrates. **Very suitable for celiacs** as it does not contain gluten. **You just have to take into account, allergy or intolerance to nuts.**

- Heath speedwell, (Verónica, en español)

"Veronica officinalis", also know as Common gypsyweed, very common and abundant climbing herb in the mountainous places of Europe and throughout America. For the curative remedies the whole plant is used, without the roots, usually in infusion for internal and topical use. Ingested is recommended pour 1 teaspoon of dessert with herbs in ¼ liter of boiling water. Rest 10 minutes, strain and take 1 to 3 times a day, warm. For topical use as rinses, gargles, poultices, washes, boil 40 gr. per liter of water for 10 minutes, strain use. **There are no known contraindications,** it is **recommended to consult** with the doctor or specialist.

- Helychrysum, (Helicriso, en español)

"Helichrysum stoechas", wild plant that grows in the Mediterranean basin of rocky areas and dry soils. With dense bouquets of small flowers that are used internally or in topical use (washes, compresses). There are different presentations for infusion, extracts, syrup and ointments. **Its essential oil is neurotoxic, only used in topical use. Contraindicated in pregnancy or lactation women, persons taking:** anticoagulants or drugs of opposite effect, in case of taking corticoids or **with obstructions of the biliary tract.**

- Henna tree, (Reseda, en español)

"Lawsonia inermis", also know as Mignonette tree, originating from Tropic, it is grown in arid regions of tropical Africa, Madagascar, tropical Asia, Australia and America, considered the oldest cosmetic in the world, used to dye any part of the body even in tattoos. **There are no known contraindications,** it is **recommended to consult** with the doctor or specialist.

- Herb Bennet, (Cariofilada, en español)

"Geum urbanum", It grows in shady places like the edges of the forests of Europe and Asia. It is used, rhizomes (before flowering) and leaves (in bloom). **This plant should not be used with iron containers. Contraindicated ingested persons with gastritis or gastroduodenal ulcers.**

- Honey, (Miel, en español)

Another exception to this book is mentioned as being produced by bees from flowers. Food advised to strengthen our immune system, excellent natural option for its antibacterial and antimicrobial qualities. **Not suitable for:** diabetics, persons with a diet to lose weight, (there are exceptions). **Contraindicated in under 1 year, may contain spores, cause of Botulism and Allergies.**

- Honeysuckle, (Madreselva, en español)

"Lonicera xylosteum" or "Lonicera caprifolium", originating from Europe, there are three edible species, north, south and central Europe, also those of Altai and Kamchatka (both in Russia). There are 14 species of wild honeysuckle. Because of its detoxifying action, **fresh shoots are used to treat mushroom poisoning.** The usual use is the infusions of the crust, or of the white flowers (they grow together with the yellow ones). There are also elaborated syrups. **The main edible difference of the berries is the color,** the almost **black or blue color, you can eat,** but the **orange or red tones are poisonous.**

- Hops, (Lúpulo, en español)

"Humulus lupulus", originating from Europe, Western Asia and North America, it is a plant that is easily recognized by the peculiarity of being climber and whose stems are always rolled to the right, grows near rivers or areas with humidity. In some persons, **flowers can cause contact dermatitis.** For medicinal remedies can use ingested or in topical use the infusion of flowers or grains, also in juice. **In excessive doses can cause:** nausea and vomiting. **The pregnancy or lactation women, before consuming, consult with the doctor or specialist.**

- Horehound, (Marrubio, en español)

"Marrubium vulgare", also know as White horehound, originating from Europe and North Africa, plant with numerous villi that give off a pleasant aroma very similar to apples. Grows wild in abandoned places or along the edges on roads or paths, at the foot of walls, on **...Continue on next page**

... vacant lots, among rubble, etc. The leaves and branches are used in infusion, is prepared by pouring in 200 ml of boiling water, a teaspoon of Horehound and some Mint about 3 minutes more. Rest a few minutes, strain and drink immediately, two to three cups a day 10 minutes after meals. They are sold in capsules and tincture **Contraindicated in pregnancy women.**

- Horse-chestnut, (Castaño de Indias, en español)

"Aesculus hippocastanum", also know as Conker tree, originating from Balkans, easy to find in many parks and avenues as an ornamental tree in the cities. They can be obtained in the form of capsules, also increams and even ointments. **Contraindicated in pregnancy or lactation women, in persons with coagulation problems, also in liver or diabetic patients.**

- Horsetail, (Cola de caballo, en español)

"Equisetum arvense", also know as Branched horsetail, originating from the northern European hemisphere, one of the natural remedies that used ancient cultures due to its properties medicinal, the whole plant is used in infusion. **Always consult with your doctor** before possible interactions if you are taking medication. **Contraindicated in pregnancy or lactation women, persons with stomach ulcer or intestine, acidity of habitual form, gastroenteritis, diabetics, with heart problems, respiratory system, hypertensive or hypotensive, with severe nutritional deficiency, severe vitamin deficiency, or some mineral essential (iron, potassium). If you are trying to stop smoking by patching, or consuming alcohol or other drugs continuously.**

Descriptions of plants letter I

- **Iceland moss**
- **Indian pennywort**
- **Indian fig opuntia,**
  see Pryckli pear
- **Indian sandalwood**
- **Ivy**

- **Iceland moss,** (Liquen de Islandia, en español) "Cetraria islándica", this lichen is popularly known as Iceland moss. Botanically, it is not a moss and it does not grow exclusively on this northern European island, it can be found in countries with cold temperatures, being located on the earth along with other mosses, in sparsely wooded mountainous areas and certain meadows. **Contraindicated in persons with gastroduodenal ulcer.**

- **Indian pennywort,** (Hidrocotyle, en español)
"Hydrocotyle", from India and China, very used for 3,000 years in the Orient. Its dry or fresh leaves and its roots are those used for curative purposes. In general, in 2 or 3 weeks of following the treatment, very good results are achieved. **In high doses (for its essential oil) is:** drug and narcotic, presenting headaches, vertigo, hypertension, respiratory insufficiency. **In topical use care** for persons with cutaneous hypersensitivity. **There are several presentations and forms such as:** infusions, drops, tablets, gels, lotions, soaps, face and body creams, powdered extract. It can even be consumed in dishes of oriental origin. **Consult with the doctor or specialist, before possible interaction with:** medication of antidepressants or benzodiazepines. **Contraindicated in pregnant women (abortive), in fertility treatment, lactating mothers, under 6 years, diabetics, hepatic, persons with high cholesterol or kidney failure.**

- **Indian sandalwood,** (Árbol de sándalo, en español)
"Santalum álbum", originating from India, considered a "sacred tree" being protected. It is used to massage the skin with its oil, at 1% maximum diluted in sweet almond oil, **in non-allergic persons it is safe**. Use with **caution patients with fungal infections** in the skin, scalp and nails, also by **persons** treated with **anxiolytics. Contraindicated in pregnancy or lactation women.**

- **Ivy,** (Hiedra común, en español)

"Hedera hélix", climbing plant of evergreen widely used for medicinal purposes, and one of the few survivors in Europe of the laurisilva flora of the tertiary era. **It can produce:** sensitization allergic rhinitis, symptoms of respiratory allergies, or in the skin, also **its fruits to be toxic:** vomiting and diarrhea. The most usual way to use is in decoctions. **Contraindicated in pregnancy or lactation women. There is a toxic (American) variety.**

Descriptions of plants letter J

- Jamaica pepper
- Jazmín
- Jew´s ear
- Jujube

- **Jamaica pepper,** (Pimienta de Jamaica, en español)

"Pimenta dioica", also know as Allspice, of the tree that grows in Jamaica, Mexico, Guatemala and Belize, and Pepper that is not, is actually a berry that collects green and dried in the sun and when dried in the sun it takes its characteristic brown color. Once dry they remember large peppers and hence their name, but it does not itch. The oil essential it can irritate the skin in very sensitive persons, to avoid, try for the first time in small quantities. **It is not recommended in pregnancy or lactation women due to insufficient scientific evidence available.**

- **Jasmine,** (Jazmín, en español)

"Jasminum", aromatic flower coveted for its exquisite perfume, jasmine tea is the most consumed in China for centuries. There are 300 varieties, some with yellow flower. The flowers are used for therapeutic purposes, mainly in infusion with green tea, although it can be made with others according to taste. **The pregnancy or lactation women can consume moderate doses of jasmine without side effects or harmful. Consumed in excess, it can present side effects such as:** anxiety, insomnia, dizziness, palpitations.

- Jew's ear, (Oreja de Judas, en español)

"Auricularia auricula-judae", fungus that grows on dead branches of Cork oaks, Elder (Edelberry) and other flat-leafed trees, has the shape of a human ear, is soft and flexible, dry is hard and brittle. Different colors, depending on the place of growth. The whole fungus is collected in the autumn months until spring. It is consumed raw in salads or cooked in soups, it provides more vitamins and minerals than any other fungus. **There are no known contraindications,** it is **recommended to consult** with the doctor or specialist.

- Jujube, (Azufaifo, en español)

"Ziziphus jujuba", originating from Asia Minor, fruit tree that holds almost any type of climate and soil. Its ripe fruits can be eaten fresh or dried for the preparation of jams. Jujube based pills are sold in specialist shops or pharmacies. **Excess can cause a headache. Contraindicated in persons suffering from hypotension.**

Descriptions of plants letter K

- **Kaki fruit**
- **Kale**
- **Kelp**
- **Kinnikinnick**
- **Kiwi**
- **Kudzu**

- Kaki fruit, (Caqui, en español)

"Diospyros kaki", tree originating to China, adapts very well to cultivation in warm climates of any continent. Its delicious fruit has excellent medicinal properties. **Contraindicated in patients with chronic constipation or after digestive surgery, diabetic or obese, due to its high sugar content.**

- Kale, (Kale o Col rizada, en español)

"Brassica oleracea var. Sabellica", also know as como Leaf cabbage, originating from North Europe, it requires a cold climate for its cultivation. It is a nutritionally dense vegetable, the portion of a cup has **more calcium than milk and more iron than meat,** with a large amount of vitamin C, K and A. It is consumed alone, in salads, liquefied, in some stews, baked, with a touch of Cayenne or olive oil, dehydrated. **Consume with moderation persons on anticoagulant medication, or irritable bowel.**

- Kelp, (Kelp, in english)

"Laminariales", seaweed is a very complete natural food that provides many minerals and vitamins, the Kelp seaweed is one of the best. It is elongated and greenish yellow, they develop in shallow waters, near the surface of the sea where the sunlight reaches them. When the algae is clearer (more yellowish or brownish color, it means that it has grown in greater depth). **There are no known contraindications,** it is **recommended to consult** with the doctor or specialist.

- Kinnikinnick, (Gayuba, en español)

"Arctostaphylos uva-ursi", also know as Bearberry or Grape of the bear, it grows throughout Europe, Asia and North America, a creeping plant that upholsters the clearings of pine and oak forests with its tiny leaves. Of half a meter high, small, oval, hard and shiny leaves, the pink flowers in the shape of bells. The berries are tiny spheres of bright red. The leaves of this plant **are used** in infusion as therapeutic property **for urinary problems and prostate** with a combination of plants. **Contraindicated in pregnant women and kidney patients.**

- Kiwi, (Kiwi, en español)

"Actinidia deliciosa", originating from China, are many its properties and benefits due to the nutrients it provides. **Because of its potassium content, it should be taken into account by persons with renal insufficiency and those who require special controlled diets in this mineral.**

- Kudzu, (Kudzu en español)

"Pueraria lobata", also know as East Asian arrowroot, originating from China, from its roots you get an extremely popular ingredient in Japan, known for its delicate texture, **It does not contain gluten,** ideal for coeliacs, and very easy to digest. In the kitchen it is used as a thickener, a teaspoon of kudzu equivalent to two tablespoons of wheat flour or a tablespoon of cornmeal. You can also drink. **There are no known contraindications,** it is **recommended to consult** with the doctor or specialist.

Descriptions of plants letter L

- Lamb´slettuce
- Large-leaved lime, see Tila tree
- Large-leaved linden, see Linden tree
- Larch tree
- Lavender
- Leaf cabbage, see Kale
- Leek
- Lemon
- Lemon balm
- Lemon grass
- Lemon verbena
- Lentil
- Lettuce
- Lilac
- Linden tree
- Loosestrife
- Loquat
- Lucerne plant
- Luma chequen, see White Chilean myrtle
- Lungwort
- Lychee

- Lamb´s lettuce, (Canónigos, en español)

"Valerianella locusta", originating in Europe, Asia Minor and the Caucasus, grows spontaneously in meadows and meadows, prairies with humidity, and rarely outside of Europe. Emphasizes its alphalinolenic acid (ALA), very scarce in the vegetable kingdom, and of tiny calories, it can be eaten in salads (more usual) or cooked. Very smooth flavor, with a certain dry fruit flavor and properties similar to Valerian.   **Continue on next page**

... **There are no known contraindications,** it is **recommended to consult** with the doctor or specialist.

- Larch tree, (Alerce, en español)

"Fitzroya cupressoides", also know as Patagonian cypress tree, originating in the southern cone of America, a millennial tree and one of the oldest on the planet, of light wood, rot-resistant, brown or reddish brown. Its leaves expel a liquid used to sweeten. For the ailments the inner crust of the trunk is used. **Use only under medical prescription.**

- Lavender, (Lavenda, en español)

"Lavandula angustifolia", originating from Mediterranean, bush of showy violet or bluish flowers in the shape of spikes, with a characteristic and pleasant aroma. The flowers are used as an essential oil or in infusion. **In topical use it is recommended to dilute the oil,** heat where it is applied, sometimes it can hurt babies and children.

- **The infusion, do not use for the following pathologies:** epilepsy, gastritis, Crohn's disease, irritable bowel syndrome, liver disease, neurological, Parkinson's, colitis.
- **Essential oil,** in breathing problems from a cold, it is applied to the skin near the neck or chest, relaxes the muscles around the application area allowing proper breathing. **May worsen symptoms of disease:** irritable bowel syndrome, colitis, Crohn's disease, diarrhea, digestive system, headache and muscle, abdominal swelling and blood in the stool. **Contraindicated with dermatitis, in pregnancy or lactation women and under 6 years.**

- Leek, (Puerro, en español)

"Allium ampeloprasum", originating from southwestern Europe to Asia, a kind of elongated onion and similar flavour, although softer and sweet, whose bulb is edible. **Excess consumption can cause:** diarrhea, flatulence and vomiting. **During pregnancy consume especially in moderation.**

- **Lemon,** (Limón, en español)

"Citrus × limón", originating from Northeast Asia, introduced in Europe through Spain by the Arabs, is a fruit with multiple properties, especially taken on an empty stomach, it is more digestible and less harmful dissolved in water. **In large amounts may cause:** heartburn, upset stomach, nausea, headache, diarrhea, it affects the dental enamel exposing it to cavities (better to drink with a straw). **Contraindicated during the first 3 months of pregnancy, during lactation, persons sick with gastritis, peptic ulcers, anemia, rickets, demineralization, bone decalcification, gingivitis, sores and cracks in the mouth or tongue.**

- **Lemon balm,** (Melisa, en español)

"Melissa officinalis", also know as Melissa, endemic plant of the Mediterranean coast, aromatic, with a certain smell of lemon. **Contraindicated the essential oil orally.** The most common use is infusion. **Inadequate doses can produce:** gastroenteritis, nausea, vomiting and abdominal pain. **Do not use with:** synthetic antidepressants, antihistamines, narcotics, or other sedatives. **Contraindicated in persons with hypothyroidism.**

- **Lemon grass,** (Caña de limón o Citronela, en español)

"Cymbopogon citratus", originating from India, Ceylon, Malaysia. **Very careful,** it contains **silica microcrystals that can cause gastric ulcers.** To consume in ingested infusion, it is better in already elaborated sachets. **Contraindicated in pregnant women and persons with intolerance to skin products, or who have periodic dermatitis and inflammation.**

- **Lemon verbena,** (Hierbaluisa, en español)

"Aloysia citriodora", shrub originating from South America where it grows wild, was introduced in Europe in the 17th century. Its leaves are used in infusion. **Contraindicated in pregnancy or lactation women and persons with thyroid.**

- Lentil, (Lenteja, en español)

"Lens culinaris", one of the oldest vegetables in history, were cultivated during the 7,000 BC, in Asia. Of sizes, colors and flavors depending on the variety, among them the red one (without skin, they cook in 3 minutes), also known as Egyptian lentil, very widespread in the Middle East. They are rich in vegetable proteins, as they do not contain cholesterol, they are an alternative to foods of animal origin. They can be eaten as a main course and instead of meat or fish. **They do not contain gluten,** excellent for coeliacs. **Use moderately persons who suffer from colitis**, in excess can increase irritation of the mucous membranes. **Contraindicated in persons with gout problems,** containing purines **can increase uric acid.**

- Lettuce, (Lechuga, en español)

"Lactuca sativa", originating from Asia, composed of shiny green leaves in rounded shape. The lettuce **has to be consumed fresh** so that it contributes all the properties that it has. The **green leaves** are those that contain **greater nutritional property,** the leaves of the interior with a lighter color contribute less medicinal substances. **Do not consume in large quantities persons with kidney problems. It is sedative and can affect the intellectual and physical performance, consumed in excess.**

- Lilac, (Lilo, en español)

"Syringa vulgaris", shrub originating from Europe and endemic in the Balkans, with a flower called lilac, which, together with the leaves and crust, possess the active principles assets used as infusion remedies. The crust at 30% per liter of boiling water. Rest for 5 minutes and drink 2 to 3 cups a day, **it is a bitter plant.** The flowers are very effective preparing a tea with a handful per liter of water. Consume at least 4 days to be effective, it takes a little more time to see the benefits that conventional treatments. **There are no known contraindications,** it is **recommended to consult** with the doctor or specialist.

- **Linden tree,** (Árbol de tilo, en español)

"Tilia platyphyllos", also know as Large-leaved linden, it grows in Europe, Asia, America and exceptionally in cold and humid regions of the northern hemisphere, in Russia they form large forest areas. It is one of the most important medicinal plants, it is used mainly the infusion of flowers, dry bracts, crust and sapwood (white part of under the crust of the tree). **It is convenient to see Tila tree,** when sharing remedies. **It is also used as an antidote,** in case of ingesting toxic substances. **Consult with the doctor, pregnancy or lactation women, heart patients, with stomach pains unknown.**

- **Loosestrife,** (Lisimaquia, en español)

"Lysimachia vulgaris", also know as Garden yellow loosestrife, originating from South of Europa, known as money plant. The juice of the leaves by the astringent virtue that possess cures the sputum of blood. Dry leaves and flowers are used, and from all its parts dyes are extracted. The most common use is the infusion of two teaspoons of dry loosestrife poured in 250 gr. of boiling water. Rest for 5 minutes, strain and drink. **There are no known contraindications,** it is **recommended to consult** with the doctor or specialist.

- **Loquat,** (Níspero, en español)

"Eriobotrya japónica", originating from China, it has been cultivated for more than 1,500 years. It is the first fruit of the spring and for its therapeutic properties can be considered medicine. It is used in infusion and there are extracts of the leaves. **Consume in moderation persons with irritable colon. Do not consume the seeds, they are very toxic.**

- **Lucerne plant,** (Alfalfa, en español)

"Medicago sativa", originating from Persia, probably adopted by man in the Bronze Age as food for horses from Central Asia. According to Pliny the Elder, it was introduced in Greece around 490 B.C. Herb with great nutritional and medicinal properties. It has more than double the protein, four times more calcium and twice as **...Continue on next page**

... much iron as most vegetables. Four times more vitamin A, three times more vitamin B complex and nine times more vitamin E, and a high percentage of vitamin K. **Do not overconsume**. As **side effects,** being rich in fiber and protein, **it can cause:** upset stomach, gas or flatulence and even diarrhea. **Contraindicated to consume capsules or alfalfa supplements, by pregnant women (abortive), or lactation. Contraindicated consume in any way, children under 6 years and persons with hypoglycemia.**

- Lungwort, (Pulmonaria, en español)

"Pulmonaria officinalis", originating from zones with temperate climate of Europe, it grows wild in open forests, oak groves, fallow land, next to rivers, streams or wetlands in general, also in arid or calcareous soils. The stems are topped with pink flowers at the beginning and blue when they open; It is common to see up to three different colors. It is used in infusion normally. There is the tincture with the same properties. **Contraindicated in pregnancy or lactation women, persons with hepatopathies by pyrrolizidine alkaloids.**

- Lychee, (Lichi, en español)

"Litchi chinensis", originating from South of China, very used in their traditional medicine. Its cultivation and consumption has spread throughout subtropical áreas. **Of reddish and scaly skin,** light-coloured pulp, sweet taste and aroma of roses. **Radically contraindicated in gout patients, diabetics, persons with obesity or wish to reduce weight.**

Descriptions of plants letter M

- Malabar nut
- Male wormwood, see Southern wormwood
- Mallow
- Mandarin orange, see Tangerina
- Mango
- Marjoram

- Marsh mallow
- Martagon lily
- Meadow false fleabane, see Common fleabane
- Melissa, see Lemon balm
- Mignonette tree, see Henna tree
- Mint
- Mountain-ash, see Rowan
- Mountain everlasting
- Mouse-ear hawkweed, see Hawkweed
- Mullein
- Muskmelon
- Myrrh
- Myrtle

- Malabar nut, (Vasaka, en español)

"Justicia adhatoda" or "Adhatoda Vasica", shrub very common throughout the Indian subcontinent, and widely used in Ayurvedic preparations. For the curative remedies everything is used, crust, flowers, roots and leaves in infusion. They are prepared in specialized stores. **Diabetics should use it with caution,** it can lower levels drastically. **Contraindicated in pregnancy women and under 2 years.**

- Mallow, (Malva, en español)

"Malva sylvestris", also know as High mallow, originating from European, it usually grows on abandoned lots, roadsides and around country houses. Of leaves similar to Geranium, which is a hybrid of his. Its fruits resemble a small pumpkin about 1 cm in diameter, they are edible when they are green. **As side effects may can cause certain persons:** belly pain, gas, colitis, constipation, stomach pain. **Contraindicated in pregnancy or lactation women.**

- Mango, (Mango, en español)

"Mangifera indica", originating from India and Indochina, its fruit has become one of the most popular ingredients for its various beneficial properties for the human body. **Contraindicated in persons suffering from kidney disorders and in diabetics (due to its high sugar content).**

- Marjoram, (Mejorana, en español)

"Origanum majorana", originating from Eastern Mediterranean basin, its used to Provencal herbs, with an aroma similar to oregano. **Fresh can cause irritation of the eyes and skin.** The usual use is in infusion, three cups a day. **Contraindicated in pregnancy or lactation women, under 6 years, persons with problems of hematuria (blood in the urine), gastroduodenal ulcers, hepatic, gastritis, Crohn's disease, irritable bowel syndrome, Parkinson's, and neurological diseases.**

- Marsh mallow, (Malvavisco, en español)

"Althaea officinalis", originating from Eurasia, perennial plant that can reach up to 1.5 meters, erect stems, conical roots of yellow color, white flowers with reddish ink. The roots and dried flowers are used for the remedies. They exist in pills, tinctures, unpeeled or peeled extracts, ointments and even cough syrups. The classic daily dose for the root or leaf is 6 grams. (consult with specialists). Infusion ingested or in topical use it is made by boiling water and adding a teaspoon of dried herb. Let to boil 3 more minutes, rest another 3 minutes, strain and drink **Contraindicated in pregnancy women and diabetics.**

- Martagon lily, (Martagon, en español)

"Lilium martagon", also know as Turk´s cap Lily, plant of oriental origin that although it extends from Portugal to Mongolia, usually grows in mountainous areas between Beech, Oak, Evergreen oak / Olm oak / Holly oak forest. **Gives off a strong smell** that can cause **dizziness in some persons.** The infusion of stems, bulbs, leaves and flowers (there are pink and White color) is usually used. It is prepared with a bulb of approximately 15 gr. pour boiling water and put in infusion for 15 minutes, strain and take three times a day. **There are no known contraindications,** it is **recommended to consult** with the doctor or specialist.

- Mint, (Menta, en español)

"Mentha", millenary plant that is found in all continents, is similar to Spearmint and composed mainly of water, fiber, proteins, minerals, vitamins and amino acids. Menthol or Pippermint is extracted from the essential oil of mint, with it a type of alcohol discovered thousands of years ago is elaborated in Japan. **Mint piperita** is usually sold, a sterile hybrid obtained from the crossing of the aquatic Mint and Spearmint, but with the same properties as the Mint. **Do not abuse the consumption of Menthol, it worsens the symptoms in persons with:** digestive ulcers, hiatus hernia or heartburn. **Contraindicated essential oils (Menthol) in pregnancy or lactation women, persons with hepatic pathologies, ulcerative colitis or diarrhea.**

- Mullein, (Gordolobo, en español)

"Verbascum thapsus", also know as Great mullein, originating from Europe and North Africa. Very characteristic plant, of dull green color with rosettes of small yellow flowers on an elongated stick of the plant, It grows any place and **its properties are well recognized. It can interfere with medications and enhance the action of anticoagulants. Contraindicated the essential oil in persons with the broken eardrum. Contraindicated the essential oil and the infusion ingested in pregnancy or lactation women and under 12 years.**

- Muskmelon or Melon, (Melón, en español)

"Cucumis melo", of uncertain origin of Central Asia or Africa. It grows in warm climates and not very humid with lots of light. There are many varieties: **Toad skin** (the most common, crust, greenish and rough, whitish pulp), **Gaul or Galia** (somewhat rough skin yellowish-green and with stretch marks, yellowish-white pulp), **Yellow, Cantaloupe or Spanspek** (somewhat rough skin of a greenish color, orange pulp), **Honeydew** (green or orange pulp). **Tendral** (dark green crust), **Rochet** (yellowish-white pulp). **Contraindicated the excess in pregnancy or lactation women, under 6 years, patients with diabetes, or persons with vesicular problems, anorexia, stress, anxiety.**

- Myrrh, (Mirra en español)

"Commiphora myrrha", also know as African myrrh, originating from Somalia and African regions. It grows in the Middle East. To prepare the infusion use 1 to 2 teaspoons of well-sprayed Myrrh herb and the equivalent of a cup of water. Boil the water and at the time of boiling add the Myrrh and let it boil 3 more minutes. Rest another 3 minutes, strain and drink. **The essential oil should not be ingested or applied directly to the skin,** diluted in clay, vegetable oil or shampoo. **Contraindicated in pregnancy or lactation women.**

- Myrtle, (Mirto, en español)

"Myrtus communis", bush originating from middle East, used in the famous Patio de los Arrayanes in the Alhambra of Granada in Spain. It is grown as an ornamental plant in gardens and parks located in frost-free areas. In medicinal uses the infusion is used, also **the essential oil** that is extracted from the leaves **can be colored:** from light to yellow, orange or yellow-green. **In rare cases they can cause:** headaches and nausea. **Contraindicated in pregnancy or lactation women, under 6 years, in patients with gastritis, gastroduodenal ulcers, irritable bowel, Crohn's disease, ulcerative colitis, hepatic, epileptic, Parkinson's patients and any neurological disease, or in the process of ethylic dehabituation.**

Descriptions of plants letter N

- Naranjilla
- Narrow-leaf strap fern or Narrow strapfern
- Narrow-leaved paperbark, see Tea tree
- Narrow-leaved purple coneflower, see Echinacea
- Nectarine
- Nettle
- Niaouli

- Naranjilla, (Naranjilla, en español)

"Solanum quitoense", plant and fruit typical of the Andes, grows spontaneously, the fruit is similar to a rounded yellow tomato, but its pulp is greenish normally and acid taste. Mature can be processed with its shell, increasing the level of benefits by taking advantage of the minerals and fiber contained in its external part. Normally it is consumed fresh or in juice, it has a positive influence on the organism just consumed, **it can ferment within a few hours** and be less healthy. **A lot of caution and prudence in persons suffering from gastrointestinal ulcers.**

- Narrow-leaf strap fern, (Calalagua, en español)

"Campyloneurum angustifolium", also know as Narrow strapfern, originating from Perú. Epiphyte plant, does not grow in the earth, is between crust and branches of other plants or in the middle of rocks. Fern species, stems and roots of the male fern are used in dressing or poultice or infusion. It exists in extract. **Contraindicated in persons with gastritis, duodenal ulcers and diabetes.**

- Nectarine, (Nectarina, en español)

"Prunus persica var. nucipersica", fruit of the tree originating from China, Afghanistan and Iran. It is a peach variety, the difference is in the skin, instead of velvety it is smooth and shiny, and tastes more acidic than it. **Contraindicated nectarine juice for diabetics.**

- Nettle, (Ortiga, en español)

"Urtica dioica", originating from Europe, Asia and Mediterranean basin, where they grow wild. It has elongated leaves, being one of the plants with the greatest advantages for the organism, it is very easy to identify in the field, by the itching and jagged edge of its leaves. You can eat it even in tortilla (before boiling twice) or stews. It is available dry (not itchy) for use. **Caution when combining nettle with medication.**

- **Niaouli,** (Niaoulí, en español)

"Melaleuca quinquenervia", also know as Broadleaved paperbark, originating from Madagascar, of aromatic leaves that provide an essential oil of relaxing and healing virtues, with a sweet and fresh camphor smell. Widely used in hospitals in France as an antiseptic in obstetrics and gynecology. Its essential oil is used topically and internally as it is anti-infectious, both antibacterial and antiviral. **Contraindicated in pregnant women, under 6 years, persons with breast, ovarian or uterine cancer.**

Descriptions of plants letter O

- Oats
- Olive oil
- Olive
- Onion

- Orange
- Oregano
- Otholobium, see Psoralea

- **Oats,** (Avena, en español)

"Avena sativa", originating from Eurasia and Africa, considered "the queen of cereals" for its content in proteins, vitamins and carbohydrates, minerals, trace elements, proteins of high biological value, iron, phosphorus, nutrients much richer than in other common cereals. **Due to its high fibre content it can cause flatulence and intestinal disorders.**

- **Olive,** (Olivo, en español)

"Olea europaea", originating from Mediterranean basin, since ancient times its wood and fruits (olives) have been used. The infusions of bark and leaves are used for their curative properties. **In topical use only the crust.** The leaves in injectables or intravenously reduce blood pressure and dilate the coronary arteries surrounding the heart. **Possible side effects:** irritant to the gastric epithelium. **Persons with gastric problems** eat only at meals. **Contraindicated in pregnancy women (unknown effects).**

- Olive oil, (Aceite de oliva, en español)

"Olea europeae", the first signs of the presence of the olive tree on the spanish mediterranean coasts coincide with roman domain, later the arabs promoted their cultivation in Andalusia. Its fruit has multiple benefits for the human body. **Excessive crude consumption can have laxative effects. Although it is a monounsaturated fat, it is not advisable to abuse, after all, it is a fat.**

- Onion, (Cebolla, en español)

"Allium cepa", originating from Central Asia, **diabetics** are advised to **check their sugar levels,** since it can affect their level of consumption in abundance, it can affect them consumed in abundance. **You can also react with medications such as:** Aspirin, anticoagulants, anti platelets, and Lithium. **It is recommended to consult with the doctor in the group sensitive to all this.**

- Orange, (Naranjo dulce, en español)

"Citrus sinensis", it is believed to originating from China and Japan, nowadays it is cultivated in temperate countrie. There is a very curious variety, the orange of the sanguine type (its pulp and juice are reddish as blood). **The consumption of sweet oranges in juice or directly has many properties.** Its fresh leaves, **boiled for five minutes** have effective substances that help improve our health. **If the juice produces gas,** take out of time or ten minutes before meals. **Contraindicated in persons with very delicate stomachs.**

- Oregano, (Orégano, en español)

"Origanum vulgare", originating from Asia Minor. An Arabic proverb says that oregano is good for everything, except for one thing, to cure death. It is very aromatic to grow in pots or in the garden. At recommended doses, oregano is a safe plant. **For therapeutic purposes are used:** the leaves in topical use or in infusions. Also as a condiment in salads, soups, fish. **The essential oil** to use in that topic **(ingested only under prescription),** tinctures, fluid or dry extracts, suppositories, **...Continue on next page**

... ointments, liniments and capsules are marketed. **The overdose can cause nervous alterations such as**: agitation, hyperesthesia, depression, dulling and drowsiness, or cardiac excitement due to the stimulating effects of its essential oil. **Contraindicated to ingest the essential oil by pregnancy or lactation women, under 12 years, anemics, patients with gastritis, gastroduodenal ulcers, irritable bowel syndrome, ulcerative colitis, Crohn's disease, hepatopathies, epilepsy, Parkinson's or other neurological diseases.**

Descriptions of plants letter P

- **Pansy**
- **Papaya**
- **Paronychia plant**
- **Parsley**
- **Patagonian cypress tree, see Larch tree**
- **Patchuli**
- **Patience dock**
- **Pea**
- **Peach**
- **Peanut**
- **Perforate St John's-wort**
- **Pineapple**
- **Plural gladioli, see Gladiolus**
- **Polypodium fern or Polypody fern**
- **Pollen**
- **Pomegranate**
- **Psoralea**
- **Potato**
- **Prunus**
- **Pryckli pear**
- **Pumpkin**
- **Purple cabbage, see Red cabbage**
- **Purple lythrum, see Spiked loostrife**
- **Purslane**

- Pansy, (Pensamiento, en español)

"Viola tricolor var. Hortensis", originating from Europe, wild plant with flowers of various colors such as white, lavender, violet, and all shades of blue. The best way to use the plant is by **...Continue**

... consuming a tea of leaves and flowers, in topical use or ingested. **Caution as a diuretic, use under prescription and medical control in the presence of: hypertension, heart disease or kidney failure, moderate or severe.**

- Papaya, (Papaya, en español)

"Carica papaya", also know as Paw, originating from Central America, It has many beneficial properties for health by the enzyme called papain, fruit with only 39 calories per 100 gr. Ii inhibits the production of estrogen so **it is not recommended for women's fertility. Contraindicated in pregnancy women and under 2 years.**

- Paronychia plant, (Nevadilla, en español)

"Paronychia argentea", also know as Silver nailroot, originating from Mediterrnean basin, it grows in rocky areas of maritime zones where there are stones, sand and abundant water. It is used in ingested infusions or, in topical use (poultices, poultices). **There are no known contraindications,** it is **recommended to consult** with the doctor or specialist.

- Parsley, (Perejil, en español)

"Petroselinum crispum", originating from Eastern Mediterranean, easily to find in orchards, gardens, margins of walls and roads. In flowering it can be confused with Cyanide **(poison),** very common in the field. Used as a condiment mainly. Stands out for its low content in both calories and fat, 100 grams of parsley provide 1 gram of fat and only 36 calories. **The consumption of parsley oil is not recommended in:** under 12 years, or in persons with delicate stomach, duodenal ulcers or gastritis. **Not recommended in case of:** stones in the kidney or tendency to form kidney stones and renal insufficiency. **Contraindicated during pregnancy women (can stimulate the uterus).**

- Patchuli, (Pachouli, en español)

"Pogostemon cablin", originating from Southeast Asia, the oil is extracted from the slightly fragrant leaves and white or violet flowers of the plant. It is thick, light yellow or brown and strong **...Continue on next page**

... aroma, It has been used for several thousand years. **It is safe only in topical use** applied applied directly to the skin. **Also inhaled in vaporizer. It is advisable to mix with other carrier oils such as:** Incense, Sage, Cedar, Geranium, Lavender or Rose. **Keep away from:** eyes, ears and nose.

- Patience dock, (Paciencia, en español)

"Rumex patientia", originating from Europe, the root is depurative and digestive in equal parts, improving numerous health problems. The therapeutic effects are notorious and, despite their name, they do not make themselves beg. To prepare the infusion is used between 30 to 60 gr. per liter. The mother tincture is recommended 25 drops, three times a day. **Contraindicated in pregnancy or lactation women and in case of suffering an episode of diarrhea.**

- Pea, (Guisante, en español)

"Pisum sativum", the origin of the green pea is related to the Middle East and Central Asia, where it is cultivated since the 8th century BC, advanced the 2th century BC, it would spread for Europe. It is one of the **recommended foods for those who can not consume dairy products.** Its consumption is recommended in all ages. **To avoid gas problems,** consume in the form of puree. **There are no known contraindications,** it is **recommended to consult** with the doctor or specialist.

- Peach, (Melocotón, en español)

"Prunus pérsica", in China it was cultivated 2,000 years before it was known by the ancient Greeks and Romans, it was introduced in Europe at the beginning of the Christian era. **It is not advisable to consume frequently under 6 years,** it can cause diarrhea and stomach aches. **Neither do persons with thyroid disease.**

- Peanut, (Cacahuete, en español)

"Arachis hypogaea", originating from the Andean region of Peru, there are archaeological records of its consumption 8,000 years ago. In spite of its bad reputation it is very beneficial for health and **...Continue**

... for multiple ailments, be it toasted, oil or cream. **Contraindicated in renal patients or patients with gallbladder problems (due to its oxalate content).**

- Perforate St John's-wort, (Hipérico, en español)

"Hypericum perforatum", very common in Europe where it originates. It grows on fresh slopes, uncultivated land and meadows not excessively humid. The whole plant or flowers are used, mainly the floral tops of the upper part of the stem. It is sold as whole fresh or dry herb for infusions and decoctions, powder or grajeas, cryogenic powder, tonics, oil, ointments and dermatological creams, extracts, hard capsules and soft, blisters. **Its results are widely contrasted** in mild and moderate depressions, **its effects are observed at two or three weeks of treatment.** This plant can replace drugs of chemical origin **with mixtures for depression with other** pathologies added. **As side effects, some persons can cause:** gastrointestinal discomfort, dry mouth, nervousness and hives, on the other hand, persons of skin or clear eyes have to avoid the sun while they take it. **Contraindicated prolonged use in pregnancy or lactation women, infants and with antidepressant medications.**

- Pineapple, (Piña tropical o Ananá, en español)

"Ananas comosus", tropical fruit very popular for removing thirst and hangover. With only 55 calories per 100 grams and a high percentage of carbohydrates improves energy in persons who consume it. Its low fat, protein and sodium content improves metabolism and the elimination of excess in the body. Minerals such as potassium, magnesium and copper or B vitamins are added to the weight loss support. **Not recommended with diarrhea, or in persons with diuretic treatment. Children should not overeat it.**

- Pollen, (Polen, en español)

Exception of the book, it is included in the coming from the plants serving in its multiplication, and by the benefits attributed from the antiquity, has led to its recognition as a product of high nutritional value. Endowed with prophylactic revitalizing and therapeutic properties. It contains all the essentia elements for life, and the restoration and maintenance of the health of the body. **The allergics should not consume pollen.** Considered a food superior to any vegetable or artificial vitamin. **There are no known contraindications,** it is **recommended to consult** with the doctor or specialist.

- Polypodium fern, (Helecho polipodio, en español)

"Polypodium vulgare", also know as Polypody fern, it develops naturally in almost all of Europe. The most common growth zone are walls, rock edges, tree trunks and similar sites. If it is collected for medicinal purposes, remove the green parts and dry in sunlight (dry storage can be kept for up to 12 months). The taste of the root is sweet (it contains sucrose), it can be used without any inconvenience as a natural sweetener. The very effective powder, should take about 3 gr. a day (distributed in different meals). Decoction is the most widespread way to use. Any dosage with alcohol content should **not be used by under 6 years** or persons **with ethyl problems. There are no known contraindications,** it is **recommended to consult** with the doctor or specialist.

- Pomegranate, (Granado / Granada, en español)

"Punica granatum", originating from Persia (Iran), has been cultivated for more than 5,000 years in western Asia. Its fruit enters the Hebrew, Christian and Masonic symbology. Fruit with a high antioxidant power, rich in vitamins and multiple medicinal benefits. Seeds, flowers, crust, etc. are used, and in many cases its juice is recommended to obtain its properties more easily. Whatever the form, it should be taken at least three months to assess its effects. **May cause:** nausea, vomiting, abdominal pain and diarrhea by excessive intake of seeds or juice, ...**Continue**

... which rarely persist, disappear in a couple of hours. **Avoid eating oily foods** with it. **Do not consume allergy sufferers. Persons with constipation should not abuse the juice.**

- Potato, (Patata, en español)

"Solanum tuberosum", originating from Andes, formerly it was believed that it was not edible, even poisonous. Today it is one of the most universal and cheap foods of which there are many varieties. It has a bad reputation, due to ignorance, when many people consider one of the first members to leave their diet when it is a loaded tuber of nutrients and a wide variety of vitamins, minerals and phytochemicals that help prevent disease and benefit our health. **Caution, with the solanine, green substance that is just under the skin,** eat the raw potato or with skin (in abundance) it can be a danger to our health, being a **natural pesticide.** It is advisable **to remove the skin perfectly and consume the potatoes immediately,** the concentrations of solanine increase the older the potato is. **It is recommended to cook the potato without skin to prevent this alkaloid can affect us.**

- Pryckli pear, (Higo chumbo o Tuna, en español)

"Opuntia ficus-indica", also know as Indian fig opuntia or Barbary fig, originating from Mexico, fruit quite unknown in many countries, difficult to collect and peel. It is used in the preparation of different beauty products such as shampoo, creams and gels for their enormous medicinal qualities. **Caution persons with urinary tract infections. Contraindicated in persons with a reduced fluid intake, serious cardiac or renal pathologies.**

- Psoralea, (Psoralea o Culen, en español)

"Psoralea glandulosa" or "Otholobium glandulosum", also know as Otholobium, originating from Argentina, Peru, Chile and Uruguay, of strong, vertical stems and some villi. The leaves are very aromatic, and the tips transparent. It can be found in dry meadows, ... **Continue on next page**

... stony slopes, abandoned lands, roadsides in crops. **There are no known contraindications,** it is **recommended to consult** with the doctor or specialist.

- Pumpkin or Calabash, (Calabaza, en español)

"Cucurbita máxima", originating from Mexico and Texas, has been cultivating for more than 4,000 years. With the exception of its roots, for therapeutic purposes **it is used in internal or topical use:** leaves, flower, fruit (pumpkin) and its seeds (pumpkin seeds). The seed does not irritate or are toxic, it can be consumed without any fear. The flower, large and similar to the bells, but yellow orange, can be coated in flour. Consuming raw flower in salads, soups or steamed, they take better advantage of their properties. There are preparations with pumpkin seeds. Its richness in vitamin E makes them important for the pituitary (development gland) and reproduction. **Avoid excess pumpkin seeds, persons who suffer:** ulcerative colitis, gastric ulcers or hiatus hernias (causes burning, heartburn), with gastritis (worsens symptoms). **Contraindicated with anticoagulant medication (produces opposite effect).**

- Prunus, (Ciruelo, en español)

"Prunus doméstica", originating from the Caucasus, Anatolia and Persia (Iran). The cultivated or the wild is a fantastic tree from which everything can be used, crust, leaves collected in spring, tender or fresh, and ripe fruits, fresh or dried fruits in jams. **Consume with moderation persons whith kidney stones, irritable bowel sybdrome and diabetics.**

- Purslane, (Verdolaga, en español)

"Portulaca oleracea", also know as Verdolaga, originating from Mediterranean basin and zones of Europe of warm climate. Known since antiquity for its therapeutic properties, but ignorance makes you despise things of enormous value and in this case the Purslane is considered by many as a weed. However, it contains Omega 3, and make it one of the vegetables richest in these essential fatty acids. Of leaves in the form of tears, dark Green color, stem between reddish ...**Continue**

... and violet, grows wild and even in gardens. It can be consumed fresh in salads or other raw presentations. Cooked sautéed or steamed. If you opt for your juice, it is recommended to drink a maximum of 100 gr. of fresh plant or 1 to 3 tablespoons that can be mixed with water or honey (over 1 year). In the infusions to ingest the fresh or dry plant is used, it is cooked for a few seconds so that the oxalic acid do not go into the water, being the usual form of consumption. Also the tea of its seeds. It exists in the market in **alcohol tincture not suitable for children or persons in the process of dehabituation** ethylic. **There are no known contraindications,** it is **recommended to consult** with the doctor or specialist.

Descriptions of plants letter Q

- **Quince**
- **Quinine**
- **Quinoa**

- Quince, (Membrillo, en español)

"Cydonia oblonga", originating from Iran and Turkey, but cultivated in large areas of the planet. The pulp and the seeds of the fruit are that possess medicinal qualities. It can be consumed raw, cooked, roasted, depending on the taste or the needs of use. **There are no known contraindications,** it is **recommended to consult** with the doctor or specialist.

- Quinine, (Quina, en español)

"Cinchona officinalis", tree originating from Peruvian Amazon. Due to its widespread use and commercial exploitation, it is now in danger of extinction worldwide. The crust of the branches, the trunk dried and the root have active principles. The infusion is prepared with 10 gr. of crust per liter of boiling water. It is advised to take 2 cups a day. It is obtained in powder, liquid extract, tincture, syrup. Quinine wine is curative (**in adults** only 1 glass a day is enough to obtain good results). **With moderation does not generate contraindications, in very high doses can produce:** vomiting, nausea, headache and ear problems.

- Quinoa, (Quinua, en español)

"Chenopodium quinoa", originating from Andes, and consumed for thousands of years in South America. It began to be considered a superfood in recent years. The seed provides all the nutrients that the body needs and adequate in all ages, **without gluten.** Once **boiled, it contains less fiber.** To boil, place two cups of water in a pan, heat, add a cup of Quinoa and a little salt, cook 15 or 20 minutes. **Contraindicated in persons with kidney stones.**

Descriptions of plants letter R

- Radish
- Raisin grape
- Red cabbage
- Red myrtle, see Chilean myrtle
- Red pepper
- Rice
- Rock tea, see Tea of Aragon
- Rooibos
- Roquet
- Roselle
- Rowan
- Rye

- Radish, (Rábano, en español)

"Raphanus sativus", originating from Eastern Mediterranean and used for centuries for medicinal purposes, it contains volatile oils that are similar to those found in mustard. **Horseradish is contraindicated in: pregnant women (capable of causing a miscarriage, and has even been used for this purpose), lactation women, persons diagnosed with thyroid dysfunction, gastrointestinal diseases, stomach or intestinal ulcers, inflammatory bowel disease, kidney disorders or disease.**

- Raisin grape, (Pasas de uva, Pasas o Uvas pasas, en español)

Used as a candy snacks or to add a little flavor to sweet and bittersweet dishes, raisins grape are one of the favorite fruits to delight the palate. **Contraindicated for persons with kidney failure.**

- Red cabbage, (Lombarda, en español)

"Brassica oleracea var. capitata f. rubra", also know as Purple cabbage, originating from Mediterranean basin, cultivated by the Egyptians from 2,500 BC, is a variety of cabbage and generally winter. To obtain its medicinal properties it can be ingested in juice, raw or cooked, in this last form the ideal is to cook approximately 40 minutes on low heat so that it does not lose its vitamins and nutrients. **Contraindicated in pregnancy or lactation women (it can develop clic in babies), persons with hypothyroidism or hypotensive.**

- Red pepper, (Pimiento rojo, en español)

"Capsicum annuum", originating from America, being known in Europe by the Spanish in the 16th century, is the most mature of peppers, can be eaten raw, boiled or roasted. **Abstain patients with gastritis, gastroduodenal ulcers.**

- Rice, (Arroz, en español)

"Oryza sativa", it is the most consumed cereal in the world, next to corn. Asia has been consuming it for more than 5,000 years. There are approximately 170 species of arable rice. China is the country that most cultivates and consumes it. Normally the rice consumed is the so-called "polished", from which the starch has been extracted of its outer layers (the most nutritious). But it is the most effective for diarrhea. If consumed in large quantities, it causes scurvy. Due to its deficiency in lysine, it is recommended to cook with vegetables, fresh vegetables or accompanied by abundant raw salad. The best is brown rice, but its appearance repels some persons. Its gluten-free protein is **ideal for coeliacs.** There is a **rice syrup** as a sweetener. **Consult with the doctor or specialist persons suffering from Crohn's disease, ulcerative colitis.**

- Rooibos, (Té Rooibos, en español)

"Aspalathus linearis", it is reality an infusion. Plant of South African origin, does not come from the same tea "Camelia sinensis". The beginning of the consumption of rooibos goes back to...**Continue on next page**

... the 17th century. Of red color, nutty and somewhat sweet, although it does not contain sugar. **Being of bipolar constipation / laxative effect, it is convenient to monitor its use in the smallest.** There is a green variety with greater antioxidant power, but very expensive. It does not contain caffeine, can be consumed at night even children. **There are no known contraindications,** it is **recommended to consult** with the doctor or specialist.

- Roquet, (Rúcula, en español)

"Eruca sativa" or "Eruca vesicaria subsp. Sativa", also know as Arugula, very common in the Mediterranean basin, its use dates back to Roman times considered a great aphrodisiac. Very versatile and peculiar its flavor, unique. You can eat raw in salads, smoothies or cooked in pestos, fillings and tortillas. **Consult with the doctor or specialist, it is rich in nitrate and can interact with certain medications, including anticoagulants.**

- Roselle, (Hibisco, en español)

"Hibiscus sabdariffa", also know as Hibiscus, originating from Egypt and tropical Africa, the whole plant is usable, there are more than 200 varieties. To make the infusion the recommended dose is 1 to 5 teaspoons of dried "flowers" (the calyxes surrounding the flowers) in boiling water. **Contraindicated in pregnancy or lactation women, persons in fertility treatments, or against cancer.**

- Rowan, (Serbal, en español)

"Sorbus aucuparia", also know as Mountain-ash, medium sized tree of European origin from Iceland to Russia, grows in high altitudes and rivers banks. Also as an ornamental tree in gardens and parks. For the remedies berries **(never raw)** are used, only cooked or in jams, there are also tinctures. **Contraindicated in persons prone to thrombi.**

- Rye, (Centeno, en español)

"Secale cereale", is the oldest cereal known in food and originating in Eastern Europe. It exceeds in proteins to rice, wheat and oats, **...Continue**

... with more limiting amino acid (Lysine), better in quantity and quality of proteins. LSD came out of a variant of this species in 1943. **Consume with moderation:** hypertensive persons, a tendency fluid retention. **Contraindicated in celiacs.**

Descriptions of plants letter S

- Safflower
- Saffron crocus
- Sage
- Salep drink
- Sanicle
- Saturn peaches
- Savory, see Summer savory
- Scots pine/Pine nut
- Silver birch, see Birch
- Silver nailroot, see Paronychia plant
- Small-leaved lime
- Solomon's seal
- Soursop
- Sowthistle
- Spearmint
- Spanish oregano, see Bigheaded thyme
- Spanspek, see Cantaloupe
- Spiked loosestrife
- Spinach
- Spiny restharrow
- Spirulina
- Stevia
- Strawberry plant/ Strawberries)
- Sugarcane
- Sugarleaf, see Stevia
- Summer savory
- Summer squash, see Zucchini
- Sundrops, see Evening primrose
- Sunflower
- Southern wormwood
- Sweet flag, see Calamus
- Sweet granadilla, see Granadia

Continue on next page

- Safflower, (Cártamo, en español)

"Carthamus tinctorius", one of the oldest crops of humanity, possibly originating in India. Chemical analysis of tissues of Ancient Egypt, Dynasty XII, they identified the safflower dyes, garlands made with the plant were also found in Tutankhamun's tomb. Traditionally used in China, it is known as "Hua Hong". The flower is used in infusion. There are extracts in oil. **Contraindicated in pregnant women (abortive), hypotensive and persons with anticoagulant medication.**

- Saffron crocus, (Azafrán, en español)

"Crocus sativus", of unknown origin, although phonetically the name is very similar in different languages. There are references of saffron dating from the year 2,300 BC. Well-known spice to flavor the meals for its peculiar aroma and flavor. Its medicinal properties are not so well known, consuming saffron in a habitual way is beneficial. **More than 10 gr. it can be deadly. Do not therapeutically consume more than 6 weeks in a row. Contraindicated during lactation and in women who suffer from metrorragia, it could cause bleeding outside of the menstrual cycle.**

- Sage, (Salvia, en español)

"Salvia officinalis", also know as Garden sage, originating from Mediterranean basin, the most usual form is the infusion, **never more than three infusions a day. Do not exceed the recommended dose:** it can be neurotoxic and cause seizures. **Contraindicated in pregnant women (abortive), or lactation, under 6 years, persons with breast cancer and other estrogen-dependent tumors, patients with neurovegetative instability, or renal failure.**

- Salep drink, (Salep, en español)

"Anacamptis papilionácea – fam. Orchis", also know as Butterfly orchid drink, originating from Mediterranean basin. In Turkey these orchids are used to make a very energetic traditional drink that strengthens health, elevating the organic defenses for when the cold climates of winter begin. This drink is called "Salep", the starch or ...**Continue**

... aromatic flour of the tubers, in particular of the wild species, "Satirión orchis" and "Ophrys holosericea". Its prepare with 4 cups of milk, 1 cup of sugar, 1 tablespoon of Salep, mix the sweetener with the Salep in a pot. Add cold milk and mix. **Instead of sugar (without any nutritional value), any sweetener can be used (see in Sweeteners).** Mix while boiling, on fire slow for 2-3 minutes, serve hot spraying with a little Cinnamon, you can add a little Starch. Salep is sold prepared, for heat and consume. **There are no known contraindications,** it is **recommended to consult** with the doctor or specialist.

- Sanicle, (Sanícula, en español)

"Sanicula europaea" or "Sanicula Elata", originating from Europe, it grows in forests and humid places in the shade. It is used for medicinal purposes the herb and the root, in ingested infusion or in topical use, it is prepared with two tablespoons of coffee filled with Sanicle at ¼ liter of water. Boil for 10 minutes. Strain and drink hot 2 or 3 times a day, for rinsing or topical use, best warm. **There are no known contraindications,** it is **recommended to consult** with the doctor or specialist.

- Saturn peaches, (Paraguaya, en español)

"Prunus persica var. Platycarpa", originating from **Persia (Irán) o China,** the Paraguayan tree is obtained by means of mutations of the peach tree. The fruit is a variety of peach with similar nutritional characteristics. **There are no known contraindications,** it is **recommended to consult** with the doctor or specialist.

- Scots pine / Pine nut, (Pino / Piñones, en español)

"Pinus sylvestris", it belongs to the species of conifers, of which there are about 150 species, originating from Eurasia. Pine nuts (edible) are used rich in vitamins A, B, E, minerals, fats and carbohydrates. The crust and buds of the leaves / needles to extract turpentine (toxic). It is used in aromatherapy. Ingested, **only under medical or specialist control** the tincture and the fluid extract. **...Continue on next page**

... More than one tablespoon can cause: a violent reaction of the nervous system and increase in blood pressure, vomiting, ulcerations. **Contraindicated in pregnancy or lactation women, under 6 years, persons with asthma, anemia, gastritis, hiatus hernias, digestive ulcers and with tendency to constipation.**

- Small-leaved lime, (Tila alpina, en español)

"Tilia cordata", originating from Europe, from Spain to the mountns and mountains of Russia and Turkey. Tree of the genus "Tilia", narrow leaf. It is easily distinguished from "Tilia platyphyllos", of broadleaf. The flowers, leaves and crust are used as a therapeutic remedy. **The best way to consume is the infusion,** up to two cups a day, ideal before bedtime, or to spend an afternoon or a relaxed day, also before an examitation, an interview. To prepare it is recommended once the water is boiled, in a cup put no more than 1.5 grams and rest. **Use only for specific cases**, not as a routine drink. **Contains tannins,** excessive consumption **over time can diminish its positive relaxing effects. Contraindicated in persons suffering from hypotension.**

- Solomon's seal, (Sello de Salomón, español)

"Polygonatum odoratum", originating from Eurasia, it has been used for centuries as: herbal tincture, ointment, tea or supplement in the form of pills. **The whole plant is toxic and emetic, its berries similar to the blueberries.** The most common form is **in topical use the infusion of rhizomes and roots,** as a poultice or dressings. **In internal use, only under prescription and medical control.**

- Soursop, (Graviola, en español)

"Annona muricata", originating from México, Caribbean, Central and South America. The whole plant, leaves, fruits (similar to the Cherimoya), flowers, stems, roots and crust are used. **Consume the fruit in moderation,** start with a minimum dose and increase each ...**Continue**

... day or week. The part with more "power" is the leaves in infusion. **In high doses it can alter the intestinal flora (constipation or diarrhoea). Contraindicated in pregnancy women and persons with heart or blood problems.**

- Southern wormwood, (Abrótano macho, en español)

"Artemisia abrotanum", also know as Male wormwood, of origin in southern Europe, especially Italy and Spain. The flowery tops are used and stems with leaves for therapeutic purposes. **In topical use** can cause contact **dermatitis. The essential oil, in internal use is contraindicated in pregnant women (abortive), or lactation, under 6 years.**

- Sowthistle, (Cerraja, en español)

"Sonchus oleraceus", originating from Europe, Asia and north of Africa, steep stem invasive grass, triangular leaves with jagged edges. Lemon yellow flowers (similar to dandelion) with numerous small heads. The root and leaves are used in decoctions or broths. The leaves as food are tastier collected before flowering, **there are packged.** The roots, when they have a certain consistency opportunely roasted and ground, serve to prepare a substitute drink of coffee. **There are no known contraindications,** it is **recommended to consult** with the doctor or specialist.

- Spearmint, (Hierbabuena, en español)

"Mentha spicata", originating from Middle East and Asia. For **under 6 years and in pregnant women** it can cause **anemia** by inhibiting the absorption of iron. **In excess it can cause liver damage.** The usual way to swallow is the infusion. **A lot of caution:** diabetics, persons taking antacids, cyclosporine, with hiatus hernia, GERD or gastroesophageal reflux disease, those medicated for the liver or hypertension.

- Spiked loosestrife, (Salicaria, en español)

"Lythrum salicaria", also know as Purple lythrum, originating from Eurasian wetlands. One of the 100 most invasive species in the world. **The side effect could be:** gastric disorder due to its ...**Continue on next page**

... tannin content. **It is avoided mixed with:** Mallow, Marsh mallow or Broadleaf plantain. **Perform short oral treatments in:** persons with iron deficiency anemia. **Taking iron supplements:** space at least two hours since the intake of Spiked loosestrife. **Contraindicated alcoholic dosage in under 2 years and in persons ethylic dehabituation.**

- Spinach, (Espinaca, en español)

"Spinacia oleracea", originating from Persia (Iran) and introduced in Spain by the Arabs in the 11th century. Excellent natural resource of vitamins, fibers and minerals, compared to meats, provides few calories and does not contain fats, when composed mostly of water. Its stems are more rich in fiber than leaves. The best way to boil wáter in a bowl add the spinach and cook 1 minute uncovered. **For a long time,** you will lose much of your nutrients. **Contraindicated in patients who have suffered from renal colic, gout, rheumatoid arthritis, osteoarthritis.**

- Spiny restharrow, (Gatuña, en español)

"Ononis spinosa", originating from Europe, Western Asia and North Africa, bush with large roots and difficult to eradicate. The whole plant is used, especially the root, with depurative benefits. **Patients with severe heart and kidney failure, consult with the doctor before use.**

- Spirulina, (Espirulina, en español)

"Arthrospira máxima" and "Arthrospira platensis", are two components of this species of algae considered a superfood against weight loss. They are not harmful supplements. **It can produce side effects such as:** thirst, constipation, some fever, slight dizziness, stomach pain, headache, itching or rash on the skin. **Use under medical supervision during pregnancy or lactation women and persons with hyperthyroidism or hypothyroidism because of its iodine content.**

- Stevia, (Stevia, en español)

"Stevia rebaudiana", also know as Sugarleaf, originating from South America, it can still be found in wild way, it is currently cultivated for consumption. It is a powerful sweetener, **has hardly any calories or carbohydrates** (1 gr. of Stevia has 1 calorie and 1 gr. of carbohydrates), **no fat or cholesterol.** The leaves contain a variety of nutrients, such as **proteins, fiber, carbohydrates, vitamins A and C, and minerals such as sodium, magnesium, iron, phosphorus, calcium, potassium, and zinc,** in processed form are not appreciated. There is a white powder like sugar being 200 to 300 times sweeter than it and leaves between 15 and 20 times. **You can use the fresh plant,** small pieces of a leaf, according to the sweetness to be desired. To be used several times in different preparations such as biscuits, cakes or infusions, Boil leaves in a liter of water and keep the obtained liquid in a cool place. **They exist:** sachets (to mix with other tisanes), dry leaves, essence, pills, liquid extract and powder. **It can cause allergic reactions in persons sensitive to:** plants of the families of Chrysanthemum and Daisy. **Side effects include:** nausea, abdominal distension and gas. At very high levels it can affect the hypotensive. **Contraindicated in pregnant and lactating women.**

- Strawberry plant / Strawberries, (Fresal / Fresa, en español)

"Fragaria", originating from Eurasia, plant used as food and medicine since ancient times. The fruits are rich in vitamin C, they also have A and B, in addition to mineral salts and many other substances. The leaves for medicinal use are collected in summer when the plant is in flower. The roots are harvested in the spring or autumn. **Consume with moderation persons in diarrheal processes, allergic to aspirin, with renal lithiasis by oxalates, with anticoagulant medication or problems to absorb iron.**

- Sugarcane, (Caña de azúcar, en español)

"Saccharum officinarum", whole cane sugar is one of the sweeteners richest in vitamins and minerals. Consider that even the excess of this sugar is detrimental to dental health.   **...Continue on next page**

... Varies the conditions **when used in juice,** consume the juice as soon as possible when extracting, it tends to oxidize in 15 minutes. Sugar is obtained by evaporating the juice of the cane by heating or lyophilization, **of all types of sugar is the healthiest to contain some minerals and vitamins when the handmade process of elaboration is respected.** The true integral cane sugar is not brown, it has a lightly toasted color and it cakes easily in contact with moisture, the others have additives and not the same as the color, nor the texture, nor its properties, by the elaboration procedure. There is cane molasses. **Contraindicated for diabetics and persons intolerant of glucose.**

- Summer savory, (Ajedrea, en español)

"Satureja hortensis", also know as Savory, originating from Eurasia, stems, leaves and dried flowers are used. Widely used in bulgarian and romanian cuisine especially for its typical dish, "Sarmale". **The essence** of this plant can be **very reactive** in some persons **and there is a slight risk of causing allergies. Special care for children. Contraindicated in pregnancy or lactation women.**

- Sunflower, (Girasol, en español)

"Helianthus annuus", originating from Tibetan mountains, grows wild and its cultivation has expanded to many regions of the world. Others place it from the center and north of America. Its cultivation dates back to the year 1000 BC, but there are data indicating that the sunflower was domesticated in Mexico at least 2,600 BC. The seeds they have a high calorie content. **In large quantities, its consumption is not recommended for persons who are markedly overweight.**

Descriptions of plants letter T

- Tamarillo
- Tamarind
- Tamarisk
- Tangerina
- Tansy
- Tea of Aragon
- Tea tree
- Tecoma stans, see Yellow trumpetbush
- Tequila agave, see Blue agave
- Thyme
- Tila tree
- Tomato
- Tree lungwort
- Tree tomato, see Tamarillo
- Turk´s cap Lily, see Martagon lily
- Turmeric
- Turnip

- Tamarillo, (Tomate de árbol, en español)

"Solanum betaceum", fruit also know as Tree tomato, originating from Andes and little known, it is found wild or cultivated throughout South America. It is medium-sized, smooth, bright and brick color or red when ripe and acid-sweet taste. It is consumed as fresh fruit, although due to the excess acidity, in many cases, mix the juice with water or milk. Also the juice as a soda directly, to do this boil 10 minutes the tomatoes with shell, without pedicle, let cool, remove the peel manually. Blend 3 tomatoes, and depending on taste you can add carrots, pineapple, blackberry, water, a little milk and sweeten to taste. Directly or raw, slice the fruit in small pieces and add lemon to taste. It is used as raw material in the industry for the preparation of juices, compotes, sweet preserves, jellies, gelatine, jams and frozen concentrates. You can find pre-prepared bags of concentrates in some Spanish-speaking American products stores. **Contraindicated in persons with skin allergies, low blood pressure (hypotensive), and suffer from hives.**

- Tamarind, (Tamarindo, en español)

"Tamarindus indica", originating from Africa, but cultivated with great success in part of tropical Asia and Ibero - America. **Fruits brown or dark coffee that look like small sacks. The pulp is an excellent condiment** to prepare dressings and sauces. Africans often mix pulp with rice. **The pulp is used, leaves and crust in medicinal applications**. It is very useful in places where it is very hot to fight dehydrations. **Contraindicated in pregnancy or lactation women and eat, if you take aspirin, for the possible increase in bleeding.**

- Tamarisk, (Tamarisco, en español)

"Tamarix", originating from South of Europe of dry areas, the trunk is covered with a crust of ashen reddish color. Of thin branches, alternate leaves light green, envelopes for the base and crowded. For the medicinal remedies the leaves and cruts are used in decoction at a rate of 50 gr. per liter of water. **There are no known contraindications,** it is **recommended to consult** with the doctor or specialist.

- Tangerina, (Mandarino/a, en español)

"Citrus reticulata", also know as Mandarin orange, originating from Indochina and China, its fruit called mandarin / tangerine is consumed. The English called it Tangerina because it came from the port of Tangier, the origin of its introduction in Europe. **Contraindicated in persons suffering from gastritis, irritable bowel syndrome, stomach acidity, hiatal hernia or kidney ailments.**

- Tansy, (Tanaceto, en español)

"Tanacetum vulgare", originating from Southeast Europe and Asia Minor, bush of aromatic leaves, divided and hairy dark green, flowers of white petals and the yellow central button. In the Middle Ages until the 17th century, in England and northern Spain its use was widespread as a remedy for all kinds of diseases. The leaves and ...**Continue**

... flowers are used in infusion, there are tinctures and essential oil. **Contraindicated in pregnancy women (abortive), or lactation, in persons with problems of blood clotting or low platelets.**

- Tea of Aragon, (Té de roca, en español)

"Jasonia glutinosa" or "Chiliadenus glutinosus", also know as Rock tea, originating from Western Mediterranean countries, from Provence to Morocco, it grows between the stones, forming a small bush of 30 cm, of small yellow flowers at the end of the stem, although called tea, **it does not contain theine, and in large doses produces vomiting.** Essential oil is sold. The usual way is in infusions, of strong smell and bitter flavor, better sweeten to taste, see Sweeteners. Drink up to two cups a day. **Contraindicated in pregnancy women (abortive), or lactation.**

- Tea tree, (Árbol de té, en español)

"Melaleuca Alternifolia", also know as Narrowleaved paperbark, native to Australia, beneficial for respiratory disorders and potent against bacteria, has anti-inflammatory properties. There is essential oil **for use without diluting in topical use. Do not ingest the essential oil,** the usual is in infusion for inhalations. **Contraindicated in pregnancy or lactation women.**

- Thyme, (Tomillo, en español)

"Thymus vulgaris", originating from Mediterranean basin and Asia, there are about 1,500 species, a very aromatic shrub of woody stems, with small pale pink or white flowers grouped in very dense clusters. The plant is recognized quickly because it gives off a strong aroma. Due to its bactericidal properties it was used in antiquity to embalm mummies. There is an essential oil, **before using it is recommended consult with the doctor or specialist.** The usual form is the infusion, ingested or in topical use as rinses, mouthwashes, **without sweetening.** Also as a condiment in stews, **little,** the taste is very intense. **There are no known contraindications,** it is **recommended to consult** with the doctor or specialist.

- Tila tree, (Tila, en español)

"Tilia platyphyllos", also know as **Large-leaved lime,** it is obtained from the broad-leaved tree and deciduous, grows spontaneously in the forests of Europe, Asia and North America, can also be found in streets and urban parks in cities around the world. The healing properties of the Tila are known since antiquity, its flowers are used, very aromatic and in cluster form. There are totally natural pills to facilitate your intake and have more control of the treatment. **It is advisable to avoid** its consumption **or to consult with the doctor:** during **pregnancy, in case of coronary disease or chronic digestive problems.**

- Tomato, (Tomate, en español)

"Solanum lycopersicum", fruit of the tomato plant and one of the most consumed foods in the world and for 2,800 years in Mexico. Since the 17th century it became known and cultivated in the Mediterranean basin, first, the yellow ones and then the red ones. Its low calorie content and its contribution of vitamin C and lycopene, make it an excellent ally of healthy cooking, even in heatprocessed products, including tomato sauce. **There are no known contraindications,** it is **recommended to consult** with the doctor or specialist.

- Tree lungwort, (Pulmonaria arbórea, en español)

"Lobaria pulmonaria", originating from Europe, Asia, north America and África, it grows on the trunk or above the fallen trees on the ground. The color can go from white to brown depending on the location. Very beneficial for the organism, the most used part for medicinal purposes are the spores (this fern lacks flowers). **There are no known contraindications,** it is **recommended to consult** with the doctor or specialist.

- Turmeric, (Cúrcuma, en español)

"Curcuma longa", originating from southwest of India, used since the 7th century BC. Yellow or mustard and specific flavor that gives another taste to the meals. It is consumed by sprinkling, rinsing, ...**Continue**

... as a dye, or for drinking (unpleasant taste, better to mask), to cauterize small wounds. **Contraindicated in pregnancy or lactation women, patients with gallbladder problems, with gastroesophageal reflux disease(GERD), newly operated (delays coagulation and cause additional bleeding).**

- Turnip, (Nabo, en español)

"Brassica rapa L subsp. rapa", originating from north de Europe and Asia, vegetable useful for the digestive system for its help in improving intestinal transit in case of occasional constipation, and is due to its fiber and water content. **Do not consume in large quantities in the acute stage of gastrointestinal tract disease, gastric and duodenal ulcers, as well as persons with liver or cholecystitis.**

Descriptions of plants letter V

- Valerian
- Vanilla
- Verdolaga, see Purslane
- Virginia water

- Valerian, (Valeriana, en español)

"Valeriana officinalis", originating from Europe, one of the most used medicinal herbs along with the Tila and Passionflower for almost the same remedies. Plant with several active ingredients used for pharmaceutical purposes, is used mainly the root and sometimes the flowers. **Do not take for a period greater than 10-12 days**. It can be combined with other plants of similar properties such as Melissa/Lemon balm, Passionflower **(under 12 years not recommended),** Chamomile, etc. Commercialized in dry leaves, prepared in sachets, pills, in addition to being one of the primary ingredients for the preparation of essential oils. **Contraindicated in pregnancy or lactation women, under 6 years, in persons taking sedative medications or those that affect the central nervous system.** Incompatible with alcohol, and in drivers **(causes drowsiness).**

- Vanilla, (Vainilla, en español)

"Vanilla planifolia", is one of the 110 existing "Vanilla" species, orchid creeper originatin from Mexico, there are more than 30 varieties, here the most used as a flavoring is described, grown in tropical areas of America, mainly. It consumes the fruit that comes out of a flower that barely lasts open for a couple of days, with an unmistakable and exquisite smell, forming a blackish pod where it keeps the seeds. Used by the Aztecs as a healing remedy, even Hernán Cortés came to know it. From the 17th century it expanded through French cuisine. In synergy with chocolate increases endorphins enhancing their properties. The usual for curative remedies is infusion, also mixed with other foods. The generalized commercializationis in branch, powder, tincture and essential oil. **Contraindicated ingest the essential oil in pregnancy or lactation women, under 12 years, patients with gastroduodenal ulcers, colitis, liver and kidney disease.**

- Virginia water horehound, (Menta de lobo, en español)

"Lycopus virginicus" or "Lycopus europaeus", they are two similar varieties in properties, also know as European bugleweed or Gypsywort, originating from North America del Norte (Virginia) and Europe, it has been used since time immemorial, a species with perennial flowers that is commonly used for medicinal purposes. Each spring the plant blooms with bright purple flowers. **Do not ingest in medication related to hormones, chemotherapy, sedatives.**

Descriptions of plants letter W

- **Walnut tree / Nut**
- **Water**
- **Watermelon**
- **West Indian cherry**
- **Wheat**
- **Witch hazel, see Hamamelis virginiana**
- **White clover**
- **White Chilean myrtle**

- White dead-nettle, see
  White nettle
- White horehound, see
  Horehound
- White mustard
- White nettle
- White pepper
- White mulberry
- Wild olive, see
  Anacahuita

- Walnut tree / Nut, (Nogal / Nueces, en español)

"Juglans regia", originating from Europe, the tree **sprout both female and male flowers.** It is used by consuming the fruit or the infusion of the leaves. **The leaf, applied to the skin can cause:** acne, eczema, ulcers and other skin infections. They can also lead to **excessive sweating of the hands and feet.** Applied assiduously **can cause cancer of the lips,** contain a substance called "jugione". **Do not consume excess nuts if you are following a diet** being rich in fat, being ideal to take weight. **Consumed in excess can cause:** skin rashes and swelling throughout the body, as well as nausea, stomach pain and diarrhea, in sensitive persons. **Contraindicated the essences and supplements of walnut by mouth, in pregnancy or lactation women, persons with gastritis or duodenal ulcers or consuming any medication. Contraindicated the nut, like an allergen, insecure in pregnancy or lactation women, asmatics.**

- Water, (Agua, en español)

70% of the human body is water, therefore, it is almost impossible that water does not have any benefit as a natural remedy, apart from quenching thirst.

- Watermelon, (Sandía, en español)

"Citrullus lanatus", fruit of a vegetable native to sub-Saharan Africa, achieved the record weight of a fruit, reaching 122 kg of weight. Its consumption has been recorded for 5,000 years, described in Egyptian hieroglyphics. **It is recommended not to ingest after a meal,** especially if it is **very abundant,** it limits the action of ...**Continue on next page**

... gastric juices being the longest and most exhausting digestive process. **The ideal is in the snack or mid-morning** fully ripe and red. All the parts are rich in useful substances, **even the inner white part** of the shell. It is advisable to ingest a little **watermelon rind**, has a good content of chlorophyll, useful in the production of blood. **Persons who suffer from colitis and gastritis, consume in small quantities, and between meals, to avoid problems of diarrhea, bloating and constipation**

- West Indian cherry, (Acerola, en español)

"Malpighia emarginata", fruit of a tree from South and Central America, and the Caribbean, is grown massively in Vietnam and Brazil. It has so many virtues beneficial to health, that we could say that it is a nutraceutical. **Pregnant women** should **not ingest it excessively**, or daily, **the baby** can become dependent and **develop symptoms of deficiency after birth.**

- Wheat, (Trigo, en español)

"Triticum", its origin is ancient Mesopotamia, the existence and final hybridization date from 9,000 years ago, there are remains in Iraq since 6,700 BC. Many persons consume too many calories, but not enough quantities foods with a rich nutritional content. The wheat germ it is a highly concentrated source of nutrients, vitamins and minerals that can help meet everyone's requirements. **There are no known contraindications, (except celiacs)**, it is **recommended to consult** with the doctor or specialist.

- White Chilean myrtle, (Chequén o Arrayán blanco, en español)

"Luma chequen", also know as Luma chequen, originating from Chile and Argentina, a very branched bush with a somewhat grayish crust, oval leaves, short and wide, all of which give off a soft fragrance, of solitary white flowers (endemic) that sprout of axillary form, and edible fruit, the stems, buds and leaves in infusion are used. **There are no known contraindications,** it is **recommended to consult** with the doctor or specialist.

- White clover, (Trébol, en español)

"Trifolium repens", originating from Europe, Asia and some regions of Africa. It is used as fodder and to decorate gardens to be very showy, of creeping stems and green leaves with some white spots, they have trifoliate shape of different sizes. Its flowers are white and it is the part that contains more active ingredients and medicinal qualities, the stem and leaves are less proportion in them. The usual way is the infusion of dried flowers, boil 5 teaspoons of coffee for 10 minutes, strain and drink. It can be used in topical use, for several days. **There are no known contraindications,** it is **recommended to consult** with the doctor or specialist.

- White mulberry, (Mora blanca, en español)

Fruit of the tree "Morus alba", commonly called Mulberrytree that the tree "Morus nigra" very similar, but this one with fruits of red color in the maturity and sweeter. Basically, the white mulberry has the same properties and use as the black one, only with the white mulberries a syrup is made that is used for colds and catarrhs in the respiratory tract, **There are no known contraindications,** it is **recommended to consult** with the doctor or specialist.

- White mustard, (Mostaza blanca, en español)

"Sinapis alba" or "Brassica alba", originating from Mediterranean, the seeds and leaves are those that possess the medicinal qualities. There are preparations for different purposes, **even a sweet mustard made** for the little ones. You can consume the seed directly, sprinkling the meals and in infusions. **In topical use it can** generate inflammations in the skin. **Contraindicated in persons with inflammation and intestinal, urinary and stomach discomfort.**

- White nettle, (Ortiga muerta, en español)

"Lamium álbum", also know as White dead-nettle, originating from Europe and very common in Spain. The whole plant is used. The young stems before flowering can be used as ...**Continue on next page**

... vegetables equal to Spinach. There are dyes for external use. **There are no known contraindications,** it is **recommended to consult** with the doctor or specialist.

- **White pepper,** (Pimienta blanca, en español)
"Piper nigrum", originating from India, one of the most famous spices and used to seasoning. It comes from the same tree as the black or pink one. It is when the grain is ripe and macerated in water, when the skin is removed the white grain appears. Rich in iron, calcium and fiber, less spicy than black In infusions, better mask by its strong flavor. **Consume with moderation peersons who suffer:** gastric ulcer, stomach acidity or gastritis. **Caution, if it reaches the lungs raw in children under 6 years, can cause death, it is advised to use powder.**

Descriptions of plants letter Y - Z

- Yam
- Yarrow
- Yellow sweet clover
- Yellow pepper
- Yellow trumpetbush
- Zucchini

- **Yam,** (Ñame silvestre, en español)
"Dioscorea alata" or "Dioscorea esculenta", originating from Africa and South Asia, it has been cultivated for thousands of years. **Considered for treatments of almost total female diseases.** The root and the bulb are used, the most common use is in capsules **(follow the indications of the specialist),** it exists in extracts or creams. **Contraindicated during pregnant women or suspects, in breastfeeding, under 6 years. Women with breast cancer, uterine endometrium, or uterine myomatosis.**

- Yarrow, (Aquilea, en español)

"Achillea millefolium", originating from Europe and the Middle East, it grows in meadows, hedges and meadow grass and is very aromatic, it used its leaves, flowers, essential oil, they exists in capsules. **In some cases topical use** may cause skin irritation. **Prolonged ingestion** may increase photosensitivity. **Contraindicated in pregnancy (abortive), or lactation.**

- Yellow sweet clover, (Meliloto, en español)

"Melilotus officinalis", originating from Europe, can be found easily in all dry and warm regions, slightly bitter taste, gives off a strong and pleasant aroma of coumarin. The nectar of the florets is as sweet as honey (hence"meli", in Greek means honey), is a claim for bees in summer. For therapeutic use the flowers are used, in infusion. **In high doses can cause:** slight narcotic effect, accompanied by headache and nausea. **Contraindicated in pregnancy or lactation women, persons with gastroduodenal ulcers or in anticoagulant and haemostatic treatments.**

- Yellow pepper, (Pimiento amarillo, en español)

"Capsicum annuum", also know as California, originating from America. Its consumption is recommended with small quantities (3 or 5 gr.) of healthy oils such as olive oil, this combination favors the absorption of the carotenoids. A large yellow pepper provides approximately 1.7 gr. of dietary fiber, which represents 7% of the recommended daily value. **There are no known contraindications,** it is **recommended to consult** with the doctor or specialist.

- Yellow trumpetbush, (Tronadora, en español)

"Tecoma stans", also know as Tecoma stans, originating from Mexico, of warm and mainly dry climates, grows around the edge of some roads in tropical forests. With leaves and yellow flowers in the shape of small bells that are grouped in beautiful and showy clusters, their fruits in the form of elongated capsules contain the seeds. It has 56 different chemical components in the leaves and flowers. ...**Continue on next page**

... Drink infusions made with leaves, branches, stems and even flowers and roots. **There are no known contraindications,** it is **recommended to consult** with the doctor or specialist.

- **Zucchini,** (Calabacín, en español)

"Cucurbita pepo", also know as Summer squash, originating in Mesoamerica where it is known as "Zapallo de verano". Composed of 95% water, it does not have any caloric content, being highly beneficial for the organism. Studies have shown that 100 gr. of zucchini only contribute 15 gr. of calories, and contains a very good amount of minerals. **They should limit their consumption, persons suffering from kidney failure, taking diuretics, and children who have stomach problems, such as diarrhea.**

Bibliography

The Bibliography for the realization of this monograph is part of the one used in the book 8256 Natural Remedies, I want to make a special mention to the following sources:

- **Atlas of the Plants of Traditional Mexican Medicine**
- **Botanical dictionary of vulgar Cuban names, Carlos A. Martínez Bayón.**
- **Dioscórides, Plants and Medicinal Remedies (Of Medical Matter), Books I-III, Editorial Gredos, Translation and notes by Manuela García Valdés**
- **The Great Book of Medicinal Plants, M. Palow**
- **Everest Encyclopedia of Medicinal Plants**
- **Magazin Agrotechnical of Cuba, each plant is mentioned independently through EcuRed**

General Index